Rightly
Dividing
THE WORD

Rightly Dividing THE WORD

Nathaniel J. Wilson, Ed.D
with Rush W. Locke

Insignia
PUBLICATIONS
Sacramento, CA

Rightly Dividing The Word
by Nathaniel J. Wilson, Ed.D
with Rush W. Locke

First Printing

ISBN: 978-0-9823912-0-4

Printed in the United States of America

For additional copies please visit: www.InsigniaBooks.com

Published by Insignia Publications
Sacramento, California
(916) 669-1100

$19.99 U.S.

Preface

A common assumption is that the Bible is not unlike many other old books. It is probably safe to say that many have little idea of its breathtaking breadth and scope. The truth is, there are no other books, old or new, like it. It is the only book which discloses that history has meaning as well as defines what is that meaning. It sorts out the events of earth and man and makes sense of them. No man or woman can consider themselves an "educated person" who does not have a serious understanding of the Bible. This volume provides a significant step toward that goal.

Table of Contents

The Divine Design

Discussion of the biblical subject of salvation is usually directed toward the salvation of the individual, the importance of which, of course, cannot be overstated. Nevertheless, when viewing the overall scope of God's universal work, one realizes that, as important as it is, salvation of the individual is not the "whole," but rather a component of a larger drama of staggering proportion, that is, the salvation of the universe itself and all that lies therein. The Bible is the story of the progressive unfolding of this drama (Rom. 8:20-23.)

Due to the breadth and scope of such an enterprise, it is challenging to attempt even a cursory grasp of that which is revealed in the Bible in regards to the divine design for creation. Like a large living puzzle, there are many pieces and events added in over long periods of time and encompassing the actions of many people in many places. Without guidance, finding the threads that make up the fabric of the "divine design" would be impossible. However, not only can a purpose be found in human history, but that purpose is disclosed in dramatic fashion in Scripture. No story, real or fictional, comes close to approaching the sheer breathtaking sweep and scale of the biblical revelation of God's divine design for the ages. History has meaning. It contains purpose (Eph. 1-3; Heb l:5.) Winding inexorably through the twists and turns of the record of man is divine intent. The cloth of human history contains a bright thread of purpose woven deeply into it. This thread is the plan of God for the salvation of the universe. The study of such is not an occupation for the lazy or unmotivated, but rather, requires a desire to understand the universal purposes of God, including one's own place in that purpose.

The Challenge:

Study to show thyself approved unto God, a workman that needeth not to be ashamed, rightly dividing the word of truth.
—II Tim. 2:15

The Greek word translated "rightly dividing" is *orthotomeo,* and is not found outside the Bible. It literally means "straight-cutting." The obvious implication is that the Word must be correctly "cut" in order to facilitate proper conclusions, which, in turn, lead to decisions concerning the formulation of doctrine. The emphasis is on the accurate and competent handling of the task. It also means "making a straight path through a difficult area directly to the desired destination."[1]

What does it mean to *"rightly divide the word of truth"*? It is significant that Paul does not say, "Study to show thyself approved unto God, a *student* that needeth not to be ashamed…" He is addressing workmen. "Workman" implies one who has not only abstract knowledge but who also is adept in applying that knowledge to concrete, real-life situations. Contemplation of the "timeless" is not sufficient. The "timeless" must be brought into "timely." This necessitates having a grasp of the elaborate divine plan and purpose. Only then can one discern methods of application to the immediate situation.

Workmen have tools. On a grand project, workmen must have in their possession a highly detailed set of blueprints, a pattern that conveys the intent and will of the designer. They must also know how to read and interpret those prints. It is necessary to understand every detail, every notation, every symbol, and the meaning of every line. Quality construction will demand that one "live in" those blueprints for hours and days—all before the first spade of dirt is turned. He/she must determine how tasks are sequenced, what takes precedence, and so forth. A timeline must be created and each task assigned a date and an estimate of the length of time it will take to complete. Each set of needs will be joined to a matching set of actions. Constant oversight will be required to insure that all parts of the project stay on target with the overarching timeline. Further, not only must the head-workman understand building, he must also have knowledge of leadership, human relations, contracts, values of materials, and values and sources of labor. In addition, one must also have some knowledge of negotiation and of the laws that govern such endeavors. Indeed, to undertake the construction of such a project without sufficient knowledge and experience is simply folly. Study must precede action.

> *Through wisdom is an house builded; and by understanding it is established: and by knowledge shall the chambers be filled with all precious and pleasant riches*
> –Prov. 24:3, 4

The "student" can stay safely ensconced in the "timeless" forever—reflecting, theorizing, hypothesizing, never having to step into the harsh light of application. In contrast, the workman is required to grasp the esoteric, the abstract, the timeless, bringing it to reality in the demanding, concrete, non-forgiving world of time. While others can discuss and contemplate interminably, the workman must make "de-cisions," that is, he must at some point cut away (i.e., "de-cise") all the possibilities except the one selected. Once this is done there is no returning. Thus decision-making is feared. To "de-cise" or "de-cide" is to cut away one option after another until only the one chosen remains. The question is, will it be the right one? Unfortunately, there is a yawning gap between where the workman stands and the guarantee of success he/she craves. The only bridge over this gap is leadership, that is, action based on decisions made. The worker who attempts to forever keep all alternatives open only succeeds in becoming paralyzed. There is risk involved of choosing the wrong one. The risk cannot be eliminated. However it is reduced or increases proportionate to the level of thorough preparation. So the question becomes, how does the workman reduce this risk? The answer from Paul is, "*Study...straight cutting the word of truth.*" He admonishes the readers to avail themselves of every opportunity to attain knowledge, wisdom, and understanding. To act without preparation in an enterprise of such great complexity is folly.

SOME BASIC CONSIDERATIONS

The Bible answers critical questions about man, his situation, and his universe. It usually does so in as simple a manner as is practical. For example, as early as the twelfth chapter of Genesis, the Bible divides humanity into three basic groups—Jews, Gentiles, and the church (I Cor. 10:6a.) From Genesis chapter 12 throughout the remainder of the Bible this division is evident. All individuals are Jews, Gentiles, or a member of the church. This is a simple example of "rightly dividing the word of truth."

From this it is discovered that the Bible, (primarily the Old Testament) directly addresses the Jewish nation. At other times Gentile nations are directly addressed, but usually as they relate to Israel. In the New Testament, the church holds this primacy of place. All of Scripture is written *for* the church but not all is written directly *to* it. The Old Testament was written primarily to the Jews. The authors wrote to Israel. They had neither intention to write to the church, nor did they understand the church. The church was hidden from these writers and prophets. It was a spiritual mystery. The first one to whom this mystery was revealed in its fullness was Apostle Paul (Eph. 3:9-10.)

Virtually the entire Old Testament is about the nation of Israel. Genesis chapters 1 through 5 describe the beginnings of human history from Creation through the Fall. This Fall was a fall from the presence of God and communion with Him. It was the result of man breaking his covenant relationship with God through disobedience, and the effect was man's separation from God physically (i.e., expelled from the garden), socially, lost communion with God), and spiritually (separated from God which equals spiritual death—Gen 2:17.) Man was thus left with a propensity for self-destruction, the inclination to sin, and the curse of sin.

Left to its own devices, the fallen but expanding human race developed as a society, which was fixated on the physical and finite. Consequently, man began attributing infinite value to finite structures and creations. This, of course, was idolatry, which is the core "sin of sins," that is, replacing the infinite God in His rightful place of centrality in human life with finite objects (money, statues, trees, heavenly bodies, etc.) and objectives (wealth, fame, fulfillment of appetites, etc.) The result was judgment by way of the Flood. Chapters 6 through 9 describe the events surrounding Noah, his family, and the Flood. Chapters 10 and 11 then describe the "post-flood" development of the human race as nations or "people-groups."

It is important to note that in the first 11 chapters of Genesis, God dealt with the entire human race in general. There were no specific "called-out" people. However, in Genesis chapter 12, this changed. Here, God called out Abram, from whom came the Hebrew nation. The remainder of the Old Testament focused entirely on Abraham's descendants, who became a nation, and their relationship with God on one side and the world on the other. Divine purpose was laid upon this nation. Beginning with Abraham, God chose this people to be the conduit through which He would convey a message of hope, joy, well being, and peace to the world. Through them would come the Messiah, the One through whom, and by whom, reconciliation would be made available for all humans everywhere.

Through the development of this nation, we will be introduced to terms and phrases that are important to recognize and also to know their meaning. These include words and phrases such as "age," "time," "times of the Gentiles," "fullness of the Gentiles," and many others.

Ages, Dispensations and Covenants
(Old Testament)

AGES:	CREATIVE AGE	ANTEDILUVIAN AGE			PRESENT AGE...	
COVENANTS:	EDENIC (Gen. 1:28-30; 2:15-17) / ADAMIC (Gen. 3:14-19)	NOAHIC (Gen. 8:20-9:17)	ABRAHAMIC (Gen 12:1-3)	MOSAIC (Ex. 19:7-9) / PALESTINIAN (Duet. 30:1-10)	DAVIDIC (II Sam. 7:8-19)	
	• THE FALL			• LAND	• KING	
DISPENSATIONS:	INNOCENCE	CONSCIENCE	HUMAN GOV'T	PROMISE (PATRIARCHAL)	LAW	
Judgement:	The Fall (Gen. 3:1-5)	The Flood (Gen. 6-9)	Confusion of Language (Gen. 11:6-9)	Bondage in Egypt (Ex. 1)		
New Promise:	The Seed (Gen. 3:15)	The Rainbow (Gen. 9:13-16) / Self Government (Gen. 9)	Call of Abram (Gen. 12:1-3)	The Nation (Ex. 19:1-6)		

(New Testament)

Birth of Christ (≈2 B.C.)

Timeline:
- Creation of Adam
- The Great Flood
- Covenant with Abraham (≈1917 B.C.)
- Law of Moses Given (≈1447 B.C.)
- Birth of Christ (≈2 B.C.)

Ages, Dispensations and Covenants
(New Testament)

AGES: ...PRESENT AGE | AGE OF AGES

COVENANTS: NEW COVENANT (SPIRIT) (Jer. 31:31-34)

TIMES OF THE GENTILES (LK. 21:24)

FULNESS OF THE GENTILES (Rom. 11:25)

DISPENSATIONS: ...LAW | THE CHURCH | MILLENIUM

Judgement:

New Promise:

(Old Testament)

Birth of Christ

Calvary (Mt. 27:50)

Resurrection and Pentecost (Mt. 28:5-6; Acts 2:1-4)

Present

The Rapture

End of Millenium

MARRIAGE SUMMER OF THE LAMB (Rev. 19:7-10)

SECOND COMING (MT. 24:30-31)

RAPTURE (I Thes. 4:16-17)

7-YEAR TRIBULATION (Dan. 9:27-29; Mt. 24:15)

Great Tribulation (Mt. 24:21)

Second Coming (Mt. 24:30-31)

Revovation by Fire II Pet. 3:4-7)

Great White Throne (Rev. 20:11-13)

New Heaven & New Earth (Rev. 21-22)

– Section I –

AGES

The definition of an "age" in theology is the same as in geology. An age is a period of time on earth from one major geological change or upheaval of the earth's surface to the next. Scripture reveals four basic ages. They are:

- **The Creative Age**—the age prior to the creation of Adam in Genesis chapter 1.
- **The Antediluvian Age**—extends from the creation of Adam to the flood of Noah.
- **The Present Age**—extends from the Flood to the second coming, or Revelation, of Christ.
- **The Age of Ages**—extends from the second coming of Christ forward.

THE CREATIVE AGE

Prior to the ages of man listed above was the "Creative Age" in which God created the heavens and the earth (Gen. 1:1.) The Bible does not specify how long ago this occurred. However, from the writings of Isaiah, some feel that the evidence is that the earth was, in its original state, created as a habitable place.

*For thus saith the Lord that created heavens; God himself
that formed the earth and made it; He hath established it,
he created it not in vain, He formed it to be inhabited.*
                                                    –Isaiah 45:18

Genesis 1:2 portrays a picture of the prehistoric earth which seems to conflict with Isaiah's statement. Isaiah declares that God himself "formed" the earth and made it and that it was not created "in vain" (Heb. "tohu va bohu.") In contrast, Gen. 1:2 states that it was "without form and void" (Heb. "tohu va bohu.") It is impossible to know with exactness the details of such an ancient time. Nevertheless since the earth was not created "without form and void" and yet is found in verse two being "without form and void," the question then arises, did something occur between verse one and verse two of Genesis chapter one that created the chaos on earth which we find in verse two? How long ago did this occur? Of course, no one knows. The age of the earth is unknown. Neither do we know what caused the chaos. We do know that, in the record of man's history, chaotic events of a global scale were often forms of purging and judgment (the Flood, renovation of the earth by fire at the time of the end of the age, etc.) It is also true that judgment only falls where there is transgression or sin. This leads to the question of whether sin existed in the universe prior to the creation of man. Scripture seems to indicate that it did.

In an unusual sequence of Scriptures, a case has been made for the idea that there appears to be a very ancient allusion to Lucifer dwelling on this earth in a pre-chaotic state and this prior to his fall from favor with God. The record of Ezekiel 28:13-17 refers to the "King of Tyrus." Like many Old Testament prophecies, the local and immediate subject of the prophecy (in this case, the King of Tyrus) is subsumed and transcended as the prophecy soars beyond local time and geographical circumstance. It places this "king" in the Garden of Eden prior to Adam's creation. He is described as *"the anointed cherub that covereth"* who *"wast upon the holy mountain of God"* and was *"perfect in thy ways from the day that thou wast cre-*

ated, till iniquity was found in thee." His heart was lifted up because of his beauty, and his wisdom was corrupted.

It should be stated again that much is not known of a cosmic history so deeply shrouded in the distant past. Many wild and fanciful ideas have been proposed regarding a pre-historic race on earth prior to Adam. These ideas simply cannot be substantiated.

Nevertheless, we do have these Scriptures such as Ezekiel 28:13-17; Isaiah 14; Isaiah 45:18 and so forth. We do believe in the veracity of Scripture, and we can read. Therefore, to ignore such plain statements seems unwise. While more than one explanation may be given for their meaning, these Scriptures nevertheless need to be engaged just as all others. Their obscurity does not negate the fact that they have meaning and are meant to be understood. That they are parting the veil and addressing a deep, dark past in our earth, is more than possible.

History certainly reveals no king who could possibly have fit this description given by Ezekiel. As is common in prophetic scripture, its statements do have a local meeting, but then transcend the local possibilities with a "word of knowledge" which provides insight into distant events both past and future. Thus, this passage is generally taken to be descriptive of Satan before his fall. At his fall, he is seen as being banished from his estate in heaven (Isa. 14:12; Rev. 12:4.) Statements also indicate that, in connection with this event, the earth was somehow made a wilderness. He, and the angels who fell with him, are seen as taking abode between earth and heaven, thus becoming the "*prince of the power of the air*" (Eph. 2:2), "*principalities*" and "*powers*" and "*spiritual wickedness in high places*" and the "*rulers of darkness of this world* (age)" (Eph. 6:12.) At any rate, numerous scriptural references seem to point to malevolent intent by Satan to permanently capture the earth, its environs, and its inhabitants. Being as Christ seeks the same thing, it is thus no mystery why earth has been locked in an ages long, deadly, spiritual struggle (Matt. 4:8-10; John. 3:16; Rom. 8:22-23.)

Whatever the cause, Scripture is clear that the earth is found, in Genesis 1:2, plunged into a deepfreeze. "*Darkness was upon the face of the deep.*" The earth, prior to Adam, was evidently covered with water. With no light/heat, a frigid Ice Age would result. The creation of dry land in such a state would certainly require a catastrophic geologic leveling event. We have no written record that dates back so far. Nevertheless, in startling fashion, Apostle Peter declares:

> *For this they willingly are ignorant of, that by the word of God the heavens were of old, and the earth standing out of the water and in the water: Whereby the world that then was, being overflowed with water, perished.*
>
> –II Peter 3:5, 6

What kind of terrifyingly violent, deep earthquakes would have to occur to wreck the pre-Adamite earth—flooding, leveling, and submerging its land surfaces with masses of water—and leaving it lifeless as we find it in Genesis 1:2?

However, while the earth was seemingly a "dead planet," it continued to evidently conceal seeds of life in its still, silent bosom. During this "winter of death," the earth awaited the "spring" wherein it would find liberation toward the actualization of its potential. How long was this period of time? No one knows. And while all is not revealed concerning God's activity in the whole of the universe, it does seem, for whatever reason, that the earth plays a primary role in the great and universal moral drama of the ages.

– SECTION II –

EPOCHAL SHIFTS OR DISPENSATIONS

As books go, the Bible is a relatively large and complex book. Written over a period of hundreds of years by numerous authors from a variety of backgrounds, it requires study and patience. Seemingly insignificant details, in ways unexpected, can suddenly thrust the reader into sweeping universal issues of breathtaking proportion. Thus the sheer scope of its content necessitates the formulation of methods for parting out subject matter in ways that the mind and spirit can grasp. The Bible itself utilizes numerous ways of doing this. Understanding these provides the student with a better grasp of the contents and meaning. Emphases may vary but the Bible, in the words of Duane Christensen, does have "discernible structure which highlights its theological meaning."[2] The most basic of the divisions of the contents of the Bible is simply its division into two testaments, that is, the Old and the New. Further compartmentalizing exists in that it is divided into 66 books—39 in the Old Testament and 27 in the New Testament. Further insight is gained when one realizes that the Old Testament books by the Jews were divided into three sections: the Law, the Psalms, and the Writings. Or, we can divide the English Old Testament books into four sections and the New Testament into four sections as follows:

OLD TESTAMENT	NEW TESTAMENT
First 5 books = Books of the Law (Pentateuch)	First 4 books = Birth, Life, Ministry, Death, Burial, Resurrection, of Jesus
Next 12 books = History of Israel (God's O.T. people)	5th book = History of Gods' N.T. people (The Church)
Next 5 books = Poetry	Next 21 books = Epistles (14 by Paul, 7 General)
Next 17 books = Prophets (5 major, 12 minor)	Last book = Last Things

A careful reading of the whole of Scripture reveals the Bible is a history of man's fall and God's provision for re-connection between man and God. The Bible reveals this as a progressively unfolding drama with identifiable major movements that advance toward a fulfillment of divine purpose. Each of these movements or transitions, which are often also called "dispensations," are truly of epochal proportion. A dispensation is a period of time in which God deals with man in a particular way as to sin and salvation. These events transition through a series of consecutive time periods in which, during each period, the application of salvation by God's grace carries features unique and distinctive to that period. The start and conclusion of each of these periods is obvious and easy to observe. Each is "epochal" in nature and rather dramatically signals the end of one period and the beginning of the next. Further, each such period is an outgrowth of, and continues to contain elements of, the previous ones.

Seven such periods are identifiable in Scripture. Each begins with great hope and promise. Sadly, each ends in human failure and God's judgment. Connected with this judgment, however, is a new promise providing hope in the next movement. Often a "sign" is given (rainbow, circumcision, baptism, etc.) which becomes a characteristic distinct to that period and sometimes carries over into succeeding periods. This cyclical pattern of promise, hope, failure, judgment, and a new hope continues to be seen as each period further unpacks the promises and intentions of divine, overarching design and purpose.

As we have already seen, the word most often used to identify these transitional periods is "dispensation." Paul uses this word in exclaiming that a "dispensation" of the gospel has been committed unto him. The word is closely aligned in meaning with "economy", or "house management", or "administration." However it is not a word with extensive usage in scripture. Further, problems occur as groups load the word with additional meanings in order to support their particular teachings, including ideas that clearly do not agree with the New Testament apostolic message. For example, many strict dispensational teaching declares that scriptures such as the Sermon on the Mount don't apply to our time (the church age), but were written for application in the Millennial period. Other fundamentalist dispensational teaching asserts that the baptism of the Holy Spirit, as recorded in Acts 2:1-4, is no longer available for believers today, that it ceased with the close of the Apostolic age including the cessation of signs, wonders, and miracles. Of course, if followed to its obvious conclusion, this proposed position would be indefensible, as the Church Age, which started on the birthday of the church (Acts 2), extends without break until the catching away of the church. With this being so, why would the experience which initiates one into the church be adjusted or changed in mid-stream? Such a notion violates the definition of "dispensation," i.e., a period of time in which God's salvation is extended to man with features consistent for the entirety of that period. Such notions lead to a mechanical dismantling of the Bible and its message. Some ideas which have been attached to the idea of "dispensationalism", but which lack concurrence with scripture include:

a. The idea that some portions of scripture, being addressed specifically to one particular people group, therefore have little or no meaning for the church.
b. There are different plans of salvation in different time periods.
c. It is necessary for the church to end in apostasy.
d. The "kingdom of God" is a totally different thing from the "kingdom of Heaven."

After a perusal of the dispensations themselves, all of these will be addressed from a viewpoint consistent with a New Testament, Pentecostal, theological perspective.

The overall result of such excesses is that some feel the word "dispensation" has been bent and shopworn to the point of losing its value. Others feel the word, from a scriptural standpoint, was never used quite properly in the first place. Others insist that the whole idea of dispensations is a relatively late theological development from the 19th century. Nevertheless, the actual epochal shifts and periods described by the use of the word certainly and clearly exist in the Bible; however one chooses to title them. With this in mind, and because no one has apparently come up with a better term to use, we will, for now, continue to use "dispensation" to identify these important periods.

The basic idea behind these epochal movements is that there is a clear and identifiable progression in God's dealings with man. This should not be construed as saying that there were different "gospel messages" of salvation. The justice of God has always, since the Fall in Eden, required—and the grace of God has always provided for and enabled—through the same two or three (depending upon whether obedience is identified as separate from faith) elements in man's redemption. These are:

1. **The Shedding Of Blood**

    This was witnessed man's admission of guilt before God and deserving of judgment. Blood, when shed in faith and obedience, symbolized God's acceptance of the sacrifice as a substitute in lieu of the death of the one who was offering the sacrifice. Even though the Old Testament sacrifice lacked efficacy to actually stand satisfactorily before the bar of God's justice, they were, nevertheless accepted because they were obediently offered in faith, anticipating the time when it would be fulfilled by a shed blood which did, indeed, have saving efficacy, that is, the blood of Christ.

2. **Faith**

   Faith in God was necessary—faith that God would accept these substitutionary sacrifices as He promised and that they would serve to stave off judgment for sin until that which was perfect was come.

3. **Obedience**

   Scriptural obedience is actually a part of "Faith" and is an outgrowth thereof. An outward obedience that is not an outgrowth of faith should not be identified as scriptural obedience. Scriptural obedience is "obedience to the faith" (Rom. 1:5) There is no salvation in an "obedience" (if there is such a thing) which is not "obedience to the faith." For this reason, salvation is always of faith alone, a component of which is obedience. Scriptural "believing on Christ" is a 'real' believing, that is, not only a believing from the mind, but also a believing which includes the will/heart, from which comes obedience (Rom. 6:17.) Through some clinical and semantical dissection, one may attempt to describe a faith of some kind apart from obedience. However, there is no such scriptural faith that does not include the human will, which, of course, responds by "obedience to the faith." Scriptural "believing" is not only believing from the mind, but it is also a believing which includes the will and heart, from which emerges a response. This response is obedience (Rom. 6:17.) This walking in faithful obedience to the revealed will of God is consistently the model of faith that we find in scripture.

The above elements are constants which are necessary for salvation in any generation or period of time. This message of salvation has never varied. However, the actions, or forms and rituals whereby God required man to meet these requirements varied with each successive period. The result is the development of an increasingly sophisticated picture of the breathtaking scope of salvation. Each period has distinctives, as well as demands, which progressively unpack divine redemption. Examples of this are not hard to find. For instance, Noah built an altar upon exiting the ark. He apparently built it where he pleased, or wherever convenient, with no restrictions or guidelines, and it was accepted. He then offered burnt offerings on the altar. By doing this, Noah obediently expressed his *faith* by the *shedding of blood*. This shed blood was God's way of "saving" Noah and his family from the judgment of death upon their lives. The blood of the sacrifice became a substitute for the shedding of the blood of the one making the sacrifice (Lev. 17:11.)

By comparison, under the Law, blood also had to be shed. However, doing this by anyone at home, or another place of their choosing, and doing it themselves, was absolutely forbidden. It was to be done at a specified place (the tabernacle), by a specified person (the priest), at a specified time (the Day of Atonement.) Anyone not cooperating with these particulars was to be cut off. In contrast to Noah's day, though the central message of salvation did not vary, the particulars of its application did.

These transitions, progressively unveiling the one constant divine salvation plan, signaled the ongoing provision by God for man's restoration to divine communion. God's purpose with man was, and is, to bridge the gap between God and man, bringing man from his present existential state back to his essential state of unbroken communion and favor with God.

Each of these progressive movements from one dispensation to another is a shift of epochal proportions. These transitions are easily observable in Scripture. Each one signals significant readjustments in terms of God's activity and man's responsibility. For example, in a comparison of Adam's relationship with God before and after the Fall, obvious changes can be seen—thus, we identify a shift of epochal proportion. A close inspection of Genesis 9 reveals another epochal shift taking place from the time before the flood to the time after the flood. With the call of Abraham, still another such major shift occurs as God again moves toward fulfillment of His plan, in this case by singling out a specific people to be the medium whereby He will reveal His goodness to the world (Rom. 9:4-5; Eph. 3:10.)

Again, a dispensation is a period of time in which God reveals the progression of appropriate methods for that time for dealing with man concerning sin and salvation. Seven such shifts can be clearly seen in Scripture. More than one title could be appropriate for each. However, we are identifying and captioning them as follows:

1. The Dispensation of Innocence
2. The Dispensation of Conscience
3. The Dispensation of Human Government
4. The Dispensation of Promise (Patriarchal)
5. The Dispensation of the Law
6. The Dispensation of the Church
7. The Dispensation of the Millennium

The Antediluvian Age

The Antediluvian Age begins with Genesis 1:3 and continues to the flood (deluge) of Noah's day. In the Antediluvian Age (the "pre-Noahic flood" age) are found the first two dispensations: the Dispensation of Innocence and the Dispensation of Conscience.

The Dispensation of Innocence

This period, identified as "Innocence," begins with the creation of Adam and extends to the Fall of Adam and Eve and their expulsion from the Garden of Eden. It is so-called due to its reference to man's spiritual state during this time prior to the fall. Man was "innocent" (without inward evil) and free from wrongdoing. This is the only dispensation in which, as far as we know, there was no provision made for salvation, other than "staying saved." The reason, of course, being that there was no need for such. However, the elements of "faith" and "obedience" were very much a part of this time.

Prior to the Fall, Adam and Eve evidently had no conscience "accusing" or "excusing" (c.p. Rom. 2:15) their actions. Thus, the Dispensation of Innocence was a time when God dealt with man on the basis of man's innocence (Gen. 2:25; 3:7.) Man was without self-consciousness and with God-consciousness. After the Fall, he was self-conscious but lost his acute God-consciousness. During this time, God allowed man to be tested in this state of innocence. Totally free from evil, possessing the power to freely exercise his willpower, and having been clearly taught the essentiality of obedience, man was tested as to how he would exercise that power.

We do not know the length of the Dispensation of Innocence. With no children being born prior to the Fall (due to the fact that all men have been born under sin, Rom. 5:12-21), this could hint that they were probably together in the Garden only a short time before they disobeyed God and fell under the curse. Also, if we assume that Satan was free to tempt them immediately after their creation, it seems certain that he would have wasted no time in doing so.

The method whereby man could stay "saved" (or under the umbrella of God's blessings) during the Dispensation of Innocence was simply to obey God's single command not to eat of the tree of the knowledge of good and evil. They "fell" only when they allowed Satan to lead them to not believe (have faith in) God. Thus, man became guilty and was condemned to die (Gen. 2:17.) The idea of the shedding of blood derives from the fact that the penalty for sin is death. Everything either has to die for its own sins or find a substitute to die in his/her stead.

The result of this dispensation is that man is tested and fails, consequently suffering the loss of communion with God. A most basic lesson is that sin always causes separation of man from God by alienating him from God's favor, and always leads to death.

God's purpose in this dispensation, as well as in all ensuing dispensations, seems to be to develop in man a tried faithfulness and a proven commitment to God, thus enabling man to be used of God in a capacity of universal leadership without yielding to temptation, self-glory, or any other form of failure in fulfilling the appointed purposes of God. Whereas Lucifer failed in faithfulness to God, God intends for man to succeed. The whole system of trial, temptation, and faithfulness, which God's people are subject to, seems to work to this end (Rom. 8:28.)

The result of man's failure in this dispensation was the same as it is in all dispensations—*judgment*. Man was cast out of the Garden and subject to alienation from God. The absolute moral code of the universe was violated, and therefore man came under judgment. Nevertheless, he was not left hopeless. A *new hope* was provided. God made provision for man's redemption from the Fall. It is here that we have the *first promise of the coming redeemer* (Gen. 3:15.) This verse also reveals an ongoing hostility between satanic forces and the human race, this hostility will finally end with the defeat of the "seed of the serpent" (the anti-christ) by the "seed of the woman" (Jesus Christ.) In providing Adam and Eve a covering made of animal skins (which indicated the shedding of blood), God was revealing to man the method whereby he would effect salvation (Gen. 3:21; Heb. 9:22.)

29

The Dispensation of Conscience

The Dispensation of Conscience derives its name from the fact that, during this time, God judged man's faith and consequent salvation upon obedience to his newfound awareness of right and wrong. This awareness was an apparent outgrowth of his conscience, which resulted from his fall from innocence. Having a personal conscience was the product of man's newfound knowledge of good and evil. In addition, the fact that covering was provided to Adam and Eve by skins of animals indicates that knowledge of the essentiality of blood sacrifice was also evident. Other than this, during this time Adam, and mankind in general, had no known written laws, but only a knowledge of right and wrong within themselves, along with awareness of how to be restored to God. Scripture often speaks of conscience (c.p. Mt. 27:3; Jn. 8:9; Acts 24:16; Rom. 2:12-15; 9:1; I Cor. 8:7, 12, 13; II Cor. 1:12; Tit. 1:15; Heb. 9:9, 14; I Pet. 2:19.) This dispensation, like the Dispensation of Innocence, began in a favorable setting that offered hope for great success but also ended in man's failure.

The first great promise of the coming Messiah was given in this early dispensation (Gen. 3:15.) Man was undoubtedly aware of how to worship God by offering sacrifices (from the example given by God of the slain animals to provide a covering for Adam and Eve.) Evidence of this can be found in the sacrificial offerings of Cain and Abel (Gen. 4:3-7.) It is possible that there was an established place of worship to which they came to offer sacrifices since the Bible states that they "brought" their sacrifices (Gen. 4:3-5.) Mankind was also aware that God mercifully drove Adam and Eve from the Garden and provided a covering for them. By experience, they also knew God's Word was true and that obedience was essential.

Man's test during this time was essentially the same as it would be succeeding in dispensations—to have faith in God and His promise of a coming Savior, and to exemplify this faith by the obedient shedding of blood offerings.

What is "conscience" other than self-awareness, particularly awareness of alienation from God? Another new awareness, the awareness of the presence of a sinister enemy, was also now a part of human knowledge. Man became aware of himself (self–consciousness) and of the fallen state of his world, but lost his communion with God (God-consciousness.) He still maintained the power of choice, even though his domination by evil forces was a real, problematic fact. And even though the dispensation ended in failure, God provides a hope in Noah's Ark.

Like the previous dispensation, this dispensation ended in dismal failure. The earth was filled with extreme violence, perversion, and an ungodly union of the sons of God with the daughters of men. Their offspring were apparently the godless, grotesque giants of Gen. 6:4.

> *And it came to pass, when men began to multiply. On the face of the earth, and daughters were born unto them, that the sons of God saw the daughters of men that they were fair; and they took them wives of all which they chose. And the Lord said, My spirit shall not always strive with man, for that he also is flesh: yet his days shall be an hundred and twenty years. There were giants in the earth in those days; and also after that, when the sons of God came in unto the daughters of men, and they bare children to them, the same became mighty men which were of old, men of renown. And God saw wickedness of man was great in the earth, and that every imagination of the thoughts of his heart was only evil continually. And it repented the Lord that he had made man on the earth, and it grieved him at his heart. And the Lord said, I will destroy man whom I have created from the face of the earth; both man, and beast, and the creeping thing, and the fowls of the air; for it repenteth me that I have made them.*
>
> *–Genesis 6:1-7*

This intriguing passage of Scripture introduces ideas that are difficult to grasp. Just who were these "sons of God"? Some hold that the "sons of God" spoken of here were actually the sons of Seth (the sons of Adam.) Others speculate that perhaps the "mark" that was put upon Cain was that he was made into a giant, and that these were therefore his progeny. However, while one of the above may be true, there is little or no scriptural background which validates either. It seems to be unlikely that "sons of God" refers to the sons of Seth because not all of the sons of Seth were righteous. Some were wicked, as were other men (Gen. 6:1-7; 1-13.) Instead of sons of Seth, ancient rabbis, as well as apocalyptic writings, taught that the "sons of God" were angels. There is more than a little scriptural indication that, as fantastic as it seems, scripture teaches that these were possibly angelic beings which "left their first estate" and became involved with human beings (Jude 6; II Pet. 2:4.)

While it may be a mystery how such could be, there are a number of things that seem to substantiate the idea that these giants were the product of an unholy union between spiritual beings and human women. That this idea may merit being taken seriously is further reinforced by the following, somewhat startling observations:

- The phrase, "sons of God" is used to identify beings five times in the Old Testament. Each case clearly refers to angels.
- The term "son of God" or "sons of God" is a special term when speaking of God's family. It is used exclusively of creatures that became "sons" through a *specific creative act* of God—never by natural human generation.
  - Adam is called "son of God" and is a special creation, not born of natural generation.
  - Israel is, corporately, called God's son, and, as such, is miraculously created.
  - The angels are called "sons of God" and are also obviously not of natural generation.
  - Jesus himself is the human Son of God, but, again, by special creation, that is, born of a virgin.
  - Finally, believers are "sons of God," "which were born, not of blood, nor of the will of the flesh, nor of the will of man, but of God" (Jn. 1:13.)
- Scripture strongly indicates that some angels evidently did commit immoral and unnatural sexual acts.

*And the angels which kept not their first estate, but left their
own habitation, he hath reserved in everlasting chains under
darkness unto the judgment of the great day. Even as Sodom
and Gomorrah, and the cities about them in like manner [i.e.,
as did these angels], giving themselves over to fornication, and
going after strange [i.e., unnatural] flesh, are set forth for an
example, suffering the vengeance of eternal fire.*

–Jude 6-7

The only incident in scriptural record which could possibly reference such an event is found in Genesis 6:1-4.

As quoted above, Jude informs the reader that angels "left their
own habitation," and committed acts akin to those of Sodom and Gomorrah. The word "habitation" (Gk., "oiketerion") is used only twice
in the New Testament—here in Jude 6 and again in II Corinthians
5:2 where it refers to a new heavenly body, or "house" for the believer.
Paul declares this new body to be of a higher or heavenly order, which
is, like the angels, on a "celestial" order (I Cor. 15:39-40.) The strong
indication is that somewhere the angels of Jude 6 willfully abandoned
the order of their celestial bodily state and went after strange or "unnatural" flesh.

Rabbinic literature connects a rather obscure verse from the elev-
enth chapter of I Corinthians to this discussion. There, Paul discours-
es on the order of headship, or authority, of male and female believers.
He makes clear that both men and women believers can pray and
prophesy equally (vs. 3-4.) Nevertheless, he is careful to emphasize
that this spiritual equality does not remove gender or gender distinctions. Quite the opposite, he argues from creation itself that this order
is permanently established in earth life. He explains that God uses a
man's cut hair and a woman's uncut hair (vs. 5-6) as a symbol of their
submission to the authority above each of them (vs. 4-5.) In the midst
of this somewhat lengthy discourse, the apostle injects this startling
statement: "For this cause ought the woman to have power on her
head because of the angels" (v. 10.) When queried as to what Paul may
have meant by this reference, rabbis affirm that Paul was connecting

a woman's submission to God with the outward symbol of this submission to God's order, that is, her non-shorn, non-shaven hair. The indication is that this signified that she is spiritually protected, i.e., has power as a result of being under her umbrella of strength. The unseen world observes that she is protected and that this protection is revealed by the symbol of obedience, that is, her unshorn hair.

This seeming aberration recorded in Gen. 6:1-4 is evidently within the realm of possibility. Scripture does not state that angels are incapable of sexual sin, but simply that they do not marry (Mt. 22:30) or procreate as man does on earth. Beyond this, however, there are further thought- provoking reasons for consideration of what, at first look, seems preposterous. This discussion opens one to sections of Scripture that plunge the reader into the unseen spirit world. For example, the Apostle Peter informs us of Christ's actions connected with his death and burial as follows:

> By which also he went and preached unto the spirits in prison;
> Which sometime were disobedient, when once the longsuffering
> of God waited in the days of Noah, while the ark was a-prepar-
> ing, wherein few, that is, eight souls were saved by water.
> –I Peter 3:19-20

Peter here seems to identify a special group of disobedient spirits and connects their disobedient to the time of Noah. When these verses speak of Christ preaching, the word "preached" is translated from the Greek word "kerosso," which signifies an announcement or (in today's language) a newscast. It is not necessarily a proclamation of joy or sorrow, but simply the declaring of what has taken place. Is it possible that here we see Christ, the "promised seed," declaring to these spirits once and for all that their plan to pervert the human race is a failure?

When Gen. 6:1-4 is observed in the context of the whole of Scripture, it seems to point to an ongoing demonic enterprise the purpose of which was the perversion of the genetic make-up of the human race, thus thwarting the promises of Genesis 3:15—said purpose being the destruction of the promised "seed of the woman." Instead, God brought judgment by way of the flood, doing away with these strange giants. The angelic fathers of these giants, if indeed such is the case, were banished to imprisonment in hell (Jude 6.) Perhaps Satan contrived to hold out hope for their liberation. However, his attempt to populate the earth with his "sons" failed. Instead, the announcement to these spirits in prison is that the true "Son" of God (Christ) has prevailed, and He will bring many sons to glory. Thus Paul declares:

> But when the fullness of the time was come, God sent forth his Son, made of a woman, made under the law, to redeem them that were under the law, that we might receive the adoption of sons. And because ye are sons, God hath sent forth the Spirit of his Son into your hearts, crying, Abba, Father. Wherefore thou art no more a servant, but a son; and if a son, then an heir of God through Christ.
>
> –Gal. 4:4-7

Scripture is replete with evident attempts to stymie the coming Redeemer who would "bruise the serpent's head" (Gen. 3:15.) Even after the flood, giants again appeared and attempted to thwart the people of God. Perhaps these later giants are referenced in Genesis 6:4, which states: "*There were giants in the earth in those days* [i.e., pre-flood]; *and also after that* [i.e., post-flood]."

At any rate, that there were truly giants in the earth, both sacred and secular records attest. Roman historian Suetonius recorded bones on display in Palestine in his day that were obviously human, but that were so large as to not be possible to belong to normal-sized humans. There were many giants recorded during the time of Israel's attempt to possess the Promised Land and the Promised Land was evidently filled with them (Num. 13:28; 31-33; Deut. 2, 3.) Then, of course, there was, some 400 years later, Goliath, and still later, his descendants (I Sam. 17; II Sam. 21.) This Goliath, mentioned in I Sam 17, was identified as being from the same family as the giants encountered by the spies of Num. 13 some four centuries earlier.

The giants after the flood were, just as those before, enemies of God's plan and God's people. Of all places, they were found dwelling in Canaan—the land which God had promised His people. The giants were there before Abraham or his descendants, ready to prevent God's plan for His people (Israel) to develop and become the fount of God's purpose in the earth.

Giants were, indeed, interesting to say the least. Not only were they large, but invariably very athletic, very strong, and very agile (due to, at least sometimes, according to the scriptural record, having six fingers on each hand and six toes on each foot.) Further, if Goliath and his descendants are any indication, they were intimidating, implacable, self-confident, arrogant, and bold, and could not be bluffed. They prided themselves in their strength and prowess. They lived on the high places as a sort of "king of the hill." And, not to be overlooked, and certainly significant, they invariably and without exception were never on the Lord's side. In every case, they are found standing against God's plans, against God's people, and against the pro-generation of the promised seed of Genesis 3:15.

Throughout the Old Testament, repeated attempts were made by Satan to guide first the human race, then the promised people (Israel), into situations that would destroy the genealogy from which the "head-bruiser" of Gen. 3:15 would come.

- Twice attempts were made to have Sarah, the wife of Abraham, either polluted or killed through the use of fear in Abraham (Gen. 12:10-20; Gen. 20.)
- Attempts were made to sidetrack Abraham and Sarah from the birth of the promised child, Isaac, by the birth of Ishmael (Gen. 16.)
- The family of Jacob was threatened with complete annihilation by famine (Gen. 12:10-20; 26:1-5.)
- The nation's destruction was attempted by the murder of all the male babies while Israel was still in Egypt (Ex. 1:15, 16, 22.)
- There were repeated attempts to have the whole nation destroyed—both by outside enemies as well as internal difficulties. (e.g., Ex. 1:11; 14:5-9, 11-12; Num. 14:10-11.)

- Destruction of the lineage, from which the promised "head-bruiser" was to come, was attempted (II Chr. 21:4; 22:1, etc.) One male baby alone, at one point, stood between the extinction and the continuation of the genealogical line from which Christ would come (II Kings 11.)
- Through Haman, an attempt was made to destroy the complete nation (Est. 3.) Attempts were also made to destroy the nation by making them the victims of captivity to Assyria and Babylon.
- Satan has, throughout history, attempted to seduce the chosen people to intermarry with heathen nations, thus destroying the lineage.
- Satanic forces attempt to destroy Christ at His birth (Mt. 2:16), and at many other times during His ministry. Satan attempted to compromise Christ's resolve on the Mount of Temptation (Mt. 4) and cause Him to compromise His mission.

The plaintive cry of the prophet concerning Christ, seeing that the Messiah had no natural sons, was, "Who shall declare his generation?" The answer is that Christ now leads many sons to glory (Heb 2:10; 16-17; Jn. 1:12-13.) When Christ's hour came at Calvary, He brought ultimate defeat to Satan and his forces. When Christ declared, "It is finished," a long trail of constant and unrelenting pressure from the forces of hell was finally ended. The "seed of the woman" dealt the "seed of the serpent" a final, fatal blow.

The Dispensation of Conscience thus ended in judgment with the Flood of Noah, which destroyed the ungodly giants so that the righteous (i.e., Noah) could continue to be the repository of hope through which the Promised Seed would come.

Although this dispensation also ended in failure, God again made provision for the future by: (a) instructing Noah in offering sacrifices (in faith of the redemption that the Lamb of God would eventually bring), and (b) providing the ark, whereby men who accepted Noah's message could be preserved safely. God gives the rainbow as a sign of his faithfulness to his covenant promises made to Noah.

THE PRESENT AGE

The Present Age (the age in which we live) extends from the Noahic flood to the revelation of Christ at his second coming of Christ to earth (Rev. 19.) Four epochal shifts of God's dealing with man are encompassed in the Present Age. They begin with the third dispensation, and extend through the sixth.

The Dispensation of Human Government

The Dispensation of Human Government is recorded in Genesis 9 through Genesis 11. This period began with bright new hope and potential. The flood had ended. The predominance of violence and perversion (which was widespread in pre-flood days) had been swept away. Noah and his descendants were given new and unprecedented power by God to determine their destiny. Into their hands was placed the mandate for human self-government and the power over the entire life-structure of the earth—plants, animals, etc. (Gen. 9:1-4.)

Genesis 9:5-6 records the establishment of the basic framework of human self-government and the human judicial system. Murder is the ultimate crime, with the ultimate punishment of death to the perpetrator. From this basic punishment for the most basic crime, the system of degrees of severity of punishments commensurate with crimes committed is established. The more serious the crime committed, the more severe the corresponding penalty. The ultimate punishment is, of course, capital punishment. It should also be noted that verse 5 refers to the victim as "brother." In a very real sense, any murder is, in fact, fratricide. The human race is integrated in such a way that each is, indeed, his brother's keeper.

Each dispensation contributes to the overall purpose of God's dealings with man. Vestiges of every preceding dispensation can be found in succeeding dispensations. For example, "conscience" does not disappear with the advent of human government. Going back even further, it is evident that man continues to retain God-like qualities (power of choice, universal awareness, etc) that were a part of his original creation prior to the Fall. In like manner, the human government established in Genesis 9 is still in force and ordained by God to the present day. The underpinnings of the present human civilization as we know it derive from these first three periods. It is noteworthy that in these first three periods, God deals with man universally. Only with the call of Abraham do we see a change from God dealing directly with the race to a mediated approach through Abraham and his descendants.

Part of the new hope and potential of this dispensation is reflected in God promising that the human race would no more be judged by a worldwide deluge of water (Gen. 9:11) and declaring that the rainbow would be an age-long reminder of this promise (Gen. 9:12-17.)

It is during this dispensation that the earth was repopulated from the sons of Noah—Shem, Ham, and Japheth, and became the nations of the world (Gen. 10:32.) From Shem derives the Shemitic (i.e., "Semitic") people of the world. This, in effect, is the historical Jewish people (Gen. 10:21-31.) From Ham come the inhabitants of Canaan before Israel conquered it. Also from Ham emerge the inhabitants of Egypt, Ethiopia, Libya, and much of Africa (Gen. 10:6-20.) All other people are classed as descendants of Japheth. This includes the European, Asian, Mid-Eastern, and Far-Eastern nations and their descendants (Gen. 10:2-5.)

Just as the dispensations that preceded it, the Dispensation of Human Government also ended with failure and judgment. Genesis 11 describes man's attempt to create a method of reaching heaven by his own ingenuity and efforts. The Tower of Babel was made to evade judgment and develop another way to heaven. This same pattern is found repeated in all succeeding man-made religions, including those that exist today.

ABOUT BABYLON

The dispensation of Human Government saw the rapid expansion of godless civilization. Records of this expansion, both archae-ological as well as biblical, are limited.

The most ancient history of mankind to this point is a people called the Sumerians. As early as 3000 B.C., ancient cuneiform reveals that these people were living in cities that were well established at that time and had obviously existed previous to these records.

Civilization is essentially the culture of cities. Thus the city of Babylon, which plays a central role in this dispensation, may have predated by hundreds of years the time of Nimrod and the events recorded in Genesis 11. The leader of Babylon at the time of chs. 10 and 11 is identified in Scripture as Nimrod, a descendant of Ham. "He was a mighty hunter before the Lord" (Gen. 10:9.) Nimrod was a mighty hunter *against* the Lord. He was a giant despot and hunted out those who opposed him. A rebel against God, his religious efforts can be traced to the founding of the entire spectrum of man-made religions including: paganism, idolatry, and the occult. It was during this time that the Tower of Babel was built.

Towers of Babel actually were probably a take-off of Sumer-ian builders which preceded them. As early as 2600 B.C. Sumer-ian builders were erecting structures of brick sixty-five feet high, making use of the arch, the vault, and the dome. In Babylon, these "towers of Babel", ziggurats, or temple-towers were used religiously. The most famous of these that is yet extant (in part) is the ziggurat at Ur. Here enough of the vast ruin survived for the archeologists to be able to reconstruct the size, shape, and function thereof. This one, for example, was built entirely of brick, the core being of rub-ble cemented with bitumen and the outer face of kiln-baked brick. A long stairway led up to the shrine of the city-god, Nanna, the moon-deity and divine patron of Ur. The skill, artistry and attention to aesthetics reveals an astonishing attention devoted to its artistic impression.[3] While the Tower of Babel has fired the imagination of man for centuries, the fact is that the tower is never spoken of apart from being connected with the city. The tower itself may have had a military use as important as a religious one.[4]

Thus ancient Babylon was the home of the Tower of Babel.

Some estimates are that the tower was some 325 feet high. "Babel" originates from the Assyrian-Babylonian word "Babilu," meaning "gate of God." Among the fragmentary notices of this period (2450 B.C.) is the portion of the inscription describing the building of the Tower of Babel and the dispersion. Unfortunately it is too mutilated to make much use of it.[5]

Archaeological diggings of other such worship structures of that time period point to a top tower containing a chapel for false Gods. Evidence indicates that this chapel was dedicated to the heavens with signs of the zodiac portrayed on visible symbols of worship. The bottom stage was 125 feet high and 300 feet square. It was built in stories or stages, each successive one smaller than the one below it. The Tower of Babel was also called the temple of Belus, or Baal, and was called Birs Nimrod by the Arabs.[6]

After centuries of nothing, excavations of Babylon began in earnest in the 17th century. Over a century later (1765) the Danish scholar, Carsten Nieburh, examined the ruins and concluded that they were of ancient Babylon. Ancient Babylon (Gen. 11, Nimrod, etc., ≈2250-2400 B.C.) and Neo-Babylon (days of Nebuchadnezzar, Daniel, etc. 500-650 B.C) were at the same site, with ancient Babylon about forty feet below the surface. More work was done from 1780 to 1790. In 1811, Claudius James Rich visited the site and studied and measured the various mounds that comprise the ruins, and collected inscriptions, clay cylinders, coins and other artifacts for the British Museum. His observations were published in 1812. In 1850 the famed Henry Layard, discoverer of Nineveh visited the site. However it was not until 1898 that the German Oriental Society undertook a full scale excavation of ancient Babylon. Robert Koldewey, and architect led a group of distinguished colleagues. Eventually a map was drawn of the ancient city, outlining major sites, including a plain known as the Sachn ("pan") and here Koldewey found the remains of the great ziggurat, or tower of Babel, called by the Babylonians, "E-Temen-An-ki, i.e., "the "house of the Foundation Stone of Heaven and Earth."[7] The area in which it stood had two doors and 10 gateways. Herodotus says[8] that "in the middle of the precinct there was a tower of solid masonry…upon which was raised a second tower, and on that a third, and so on up to eight." A tablet translated by George Smith[9], supplies the dimensions of all the stages of this tower, with the exception of the sixth, which is probably due to inadvertence on the part of the scribe. Scheil has published the text in the *Memoires de l'Institut*, Vol. xxxix.[10] According to it:

- Stage 1 was 300 feet square and 110 feet high
- Stage 2 was 260 feet square and 60 feet high
- Stage 3 was 200 feet square and 20 feet high
- Stage 4 was 170 feet square and 20 feet high
- Stage 5 was 140 feet square and 20 feet high
- Stage 6 was (omitted on the Tablet)
- Stage 7 was 80 ft. x 70 ft. and 50 feet high

Assuming that the height of Stage 6 was the same as that of nos. 3, 4, and 5, the tower was 300' high with its bottom stage 300'x300' square. This was the Temple of Bel and in it was the Statue of the god. The ancient Tower of Babel was identified.

Also in the city was a temple called "Esagila." The gods Bel and Nebu were carried here in an annual religious festival. (Is. 46:1-2.) Adjacent to this temple was another tower called "E-ur-imin-an-ki." This building was in 7 stages, like the Tower of Babel, and Rawlinson stated that each stage was dedicated to a planet, and had a different color. Specimens of colored inlay from this building were presented to the British Museum in the early 20th century. All that now remains of the zikkurat is a mass of semi-vitrified brickwork about 35 feet high; the total height when built has been calculated to be 153.5 feet.[11] It is not a stretch to assume that each stage of the Tower of Babel had similar heathen and cultic symbolism as did this tower, which, in itself, has credible adherents which identify this as the authentic Tower of Babel. Existence of these accounts is certain. Hundreds of seals which depict them are found in museums throughout Europe, some as old as 2000 B.C., down to 1500 B.C.[12]

The cult of Tammu, which became attached to Nimrod, was already old in Sumerian times, and he was honored. The texts do not resolve whether he was killed by the fiery love of Ishtar, or, like Adonis, by a boar's tusk. He allegedly went down to the underworld, and while he was gone calamities took place on the earth, and thus the women wept for him (Ezek. 8:14, c.p. "hot cross buns.") The gods were many, numbering into the hundreds. From first to last the attributes and characters of the gods remained practically unchanged for 3,000 years.[13] Other facts which, by archaeological work, have been discovered concerning the citizens of ancient Babylon:

- They were firm believers in the power of magic.[14]
- They had numerous incantations, rituals, idols, figures, amulets to ward off evil spirits.[15]
- The populace also had a great fear of wizards, warlocks, and witches.[16] People feared the Evil eye, the evil spell, white magic, and black magic. Animal body parts—especially the sheep's liver (Ez. 21:21) were used in attempts to induce magical healings and incantations.
- Priests gave answers by watching the behavior of the figure he was burning, or the knots in a string which he was untying, or by the appearance of the entrails of the sacrifice which he had offered up on behalf of the suppliant.
- The many Omen texts and omens tabulate into the thousands. Omens were derived from the sun, moon, stars, and planets. Here were the founders of the pseudo-science of astrology.[17]

Koldewey found that the walls of the ancient city were at least 40' wide, wide enough to ride four chariots abreast as Herodotus declared centuries earlier. Further discoveries on a broader scale in the general areas of such antiquity have, in the last 25 years, added additional information. Despite this work large portions of the ancient city remain untouched, and, except for limited work done by Heinrich Lenzen, remains so to this day.[18] It is important to keep in mind that, up to this time, not only was there only one race and language, but also only one visible form of religion. This cultic form of religion, built around the signs of the zodiac and other visible images of worship, was the central focus of unity among the nations of the world, which are listed in Genesis 10. The fact that the Tower of Babel was, in that day, defined as "the house of the foundation stone of heaven and earth" is very revealing of the religious primacy of place the Tower was given in the minds of the people. This agrees with the biblical record and reinforces the fact that the origin of manmade religion can be traced to the Tower.

Babylon thus developed as a center that became the origination point of all nations. Prior to the scattering of the nations and the confusion of language, the religion of Nimrod instilled in the entire human race basic precepts of a false religious system that continue to permeate world systems to the present time. It was here that the Babylonian cult was invented, from which have been taken elements in the creation of false religions worldwide. Here was built "mystery Babylon," the name used in Scripture for false religion (Rev. 17.) From Ancient Babylon and the Tower of Babel, the tentacles of Nimrod's system of counterfeit religion reached into every nation. Here again we see the Tower as a pervasive template for false religions replicated throughout history.

The Babylonian cult claimed the very highest of wisdom. Before being a member, it appears that one had to "confess" to a priest, thereby falling under his control from that point forward. Once admitted, they were brethren of a mystical brotherhood of man and the Fatherhood of God, a teaching that we all are the children of God from natural birth. This doctrine remains to this day in a variety of groups.

Scripture identifies the enigmatic "Nimrod" as the leader of idolatrous Babel. Ancient seals, do, in fact, reveal a Nimrod of that time. Nimrod, Izdubar, a famous hunter, who claimed descent from a long line of kings. He delivers his country from foreign invaders, slaying the usurper.[19]

He then extended his empire into Assyria, which he colonized, and founded Nineveh. However, although there are numerous similarities, that the Nimrod of the Bible is the Nimrod Izduhar found in Babylonian cuneiform cannot be guaranteed with absolute certainty.

Nimrod himself was the primary man who was worshipped. There is also some evidence that Nimrod very well may have married his own mother, Semiramis. As before mentioned, Nimrod was thought to have been killed by a wild boar. After his death, Semiramis announced that her dead husband (son) was now officially a god and that she was a goddess. She proclaimed that he was born miraculously, that he had risen from the dead, and that she was the Queen of Heaven.

Nimrod was connected and identified with Baal, the Sun God. Baal was also known as the Winged One. Other names in other nations and empires also became attached to him. In Asia, his identity was connected with Deious. In pagan Rome, the identity was as the Boy, Jupiter. In ancient Greece, he was known as the God of Revelry, or Bacchus. He was also known as Orion (the constellation), the Boy, Plutus, Aphrodite, and Eros. In India he was known as Iswara. In Egypt, he became Isis, Tammuz, Osiris as the child, and Horus the Sun God.

The pervasive influence of this ancient culture has many manifestations in our present society, including the all-seeing eye of the Freemasons, which derives from Horus the Sun God. This eye can be found at the top of the pyramid printed on the back of a United States one-dollar bill. This is called the Eye of Horus. Many such examples can be sighted. All are take-offs from the origination point of the ancient Babylonian cultic mystery religion.

Semiramis also evidently assumed different names and titles throughout the centuries. In pagan Rome, she is connected with the Goddess Mother Cybele, and in China as the holy mother Shing Moo. In Ephesus, she was known as Diana. She was also known as the goddess mother Isi. In Italy, Venus and Cupid are identified as take-offs of the original Babylonian cultic personage of Semiramis. In religious Rome, this influence is seen in the elevation of Mary the mother of Jesus to godlike status.

This system evidently included not only symbols and rituals that were passed down, but also is portrayed in scripture as the continuing haunt of spiritual, intellectual, and emotional powers hostile to the well being of the human race, and will remain so until the end of the age (Rev. 17 and 18.)

Idolatrous to the core, this dispensation came under judgment in the form of the confounding of languages, thus making normal daily communication in the course of life impossible and causing each language group to coalesce with their own. Thus where idolatrous attempts to reach God brings division of tongues, God's attempt to reach man, as recorded at the birthday of the church, brings a unity of tongues (Acts 2:1-4.)

The primary characteristic of the dispensation is man's freedom and responsibility to self-govern. Springing from Noah, who was a worshipper of the one true God, they were undoubtedly aware of their obligation to glorify the one true God. Instead, they used their newly discovered freedom and power for self-glorification and idolatry, thus ushering in the judgment of God.

The Dispensation of Promise

The Dispensation of Promise is also known as the Dispensation of Family (i.e., Abraham's family) or the Patriarchal Dispensation. It lasted a period of 430 years (Ex. 12:40; Gal. 3:14-17), beginning with the call of Abraham (Gen. 12:1-3) and ending with bondage and slavery in Egypt. Prior to Abraham (Gen. 12:1) and his call, the bloodline of Christ can be found coming from Seth (Lk. 3:23-38), the son of Adam. However, the scriptural promises of the coming of Christ through a particular people or nation began with Abraham, the father of the chosen nation.

As with the previous dispensations, the Dispensation of Promise opened with hope and opportunity burning brightly. In this dispensation are many promises of the coming Redeemer, beginning with Abraham (Gen. 12:3; 17:19), Isaac (Gen. 26:3-4), Jacob (Gen. 28:3-4), and the blessing placed on Judah by prophecy (Gen. 49:8-12.)

As has been observed, the basic laws of human government were instituted in the Dispensation of Human Government. From those beginnings, an expansion of further laws and guidelines for human conduct were established in the Dispensation of Promise. Examples of specific applications of these laws are given in this dispensation. These include laws concerning:

- Monogamy (Gen. 12:18)
- Adultery (Gen. 20:3-9)
- Priesthood (Gen. 14:18)
- Tithes (Gen. 14:20; 28:22)
- Circumcision (Gen. 17:10)
- Fornication (Gen. 34:7)
- Idolatry (Gen. 31:32)
- Mixed Marriages (Gen. 34:14)

The broad, general laws for human civilization (given by God in the previous dispensation) were now given scores of specific applications in this newly emerging dispensation. As society grew, these increasingly specific applications necessarily became more complex.

In this period God directed His personal attention to a specific man (Abraham) and his family. To them God gave explicit promises and covenants of blessing. These blessings were given to them in order that through them the nations of the earth would also receive the blessings of communion with God. This was their mission. This was their purpose. They were to be consecrated to God and live lives separate from the immoral and self-seeking practices of the nations about them. Belonging to Jehovah, they were not their own, but were a people consecrated to carrying out God's purposes.

Abraham was instructed to "come out" from his former dwelling place and to remain separate from the lifestyle and influence of heathen nations. He and his descendants were to live for God and for His purpose—to reveal God to the entire human race. God intended Abraham and his seed to be the repository of God's blessings on earth, and through them He would demonstrate His goodness and His blessings—spiritual, physical, and material—to the world. They were to be a witness to all other nations of God's goodness and expectations. This "people" was also the vehicle through which God promised the coming Messiah. Abraham and his descendants (Israel) were the medium through which God would fulfill His promise concerning the "seed of the woman," thus delivering a fatal blow to the seed of the evil one.

God not only called Abraham out of his homeland (Gen. 12:1-3) but also led him to a specific land—Canaan. Why did God choose this land? While we may not be able to completely answer this question, it was, nevertheless, perfectly situated for being the world capital. With Asia and India to the east, Europe to the north and west, and Africa to the south, it was central to much of the world. Being located on the Mediterranean Sea gave easy sea access from the west. It was, and is, literally the crossroads of the world. Thus, it was God's ordained purpose to establish His earthly people of Israel there. God's plan and purpose was to be fulfilled in this land, and there was to be the birthplace of both the "seed of the woman" and the place from which He would rule all nations forever.

No doubt, Abraham had little concept of all that God had in store for him following his call out of Ur of the Chaldees. Nevertheless, Abraham journeyed by faith in obedience to the divine summons (Heb. 11:8.) Departing his own country he goes to dwell in a land promised to him–a land occupied by giants. Here God would give him revelation that would be of universal consequence.

When walking according to divine direction, the Israelites were an example to all nations of the power of God over evil, sickness, poverty, bondage, and sin. At times, the whole nation was healthy, with none feeble among them (Ps. 105:37; 107:20.)

However this dispensation, like the preceding ones, ultimately closed in failure and judgment. Each succeeding patriarch following Abraham (i.e., Isaac, Jacob, Jacob's twelve sons, etc.) possessed less experience and power with God than did his forefathers. Their character and destiny finally bottomed out with the selling of Joseph into slavery in Egypt, the final result of which was bondage and slavery (Ex. 1:7-14.) Becoming unbearable, this oppression eventually caused the people to cry mightily to God for deliverance (Ex. 2:23-24.) In answer, God sent Moses, who led them out of Egypt. This led to the Dispensation of Law.

The Dispensation of Law

The Dispensation of Law began with the children of Israel's exodus from Egypt and receiving the law at Sinai. Its conclusion came with the announcement of the coming of the Kingdom of Heaven (announced by John the Baptist and culminating at Calvary.) The name of the dispensation derives from God's giving of his law to Israel at Sinai.

It should be noted that all dispensations do not end abruptly. Sometimes, as in the case of the movement from the Dispensation of Law to the Dispensation of Grace, the transition is not sudden but gradual. For example, Matthew 11:13 tells us that "*all the prophets and the law prophesied until John.*" However, the era, or dispensation, called Grace, in the most exact sense, actually begins with the outpouring of the Holy Spirit in Acts 2:1-4.

The call of Moses establishes a model that reveals the divine method in effecting the deliverance and guidance of the chosen people. This method of operation recurs again and again. As God delivers and leads his people, He chooses an individual to lead. He then ordains, commissions, and stands behind that individual as he follows God's leading. The secret to the success of each successive leader is anointing by the Spirit (Num. 11:17, 25.) This pattern is deeply engrained in scripture and transfers from Moses to Joshua, then to the Judges, then Samuel, and moves forward to, and rests upon Saul, David, Solomon, and the prophets. In like seamless manner the New Testament begins with, "*There was a man sent from God, whose name was John*" (John 1:6.) Christ Himself, who is also anointed at his baptism and ensuing initiation in the high wilderness, succeeds John. His first statement after returning home from said anointing is "*He hath anointed me...*" (Lk. 4:18.) Jesus then transfers this anointing to Peter and the apostles (Jn. 20:22) and those Spirit baptized at Pentecost (Acts 2:1-4.) Finally, the whole body is anointed to be leaders in proclaiming the gospel, led by the five-fold ministry (Eph. 4:7-11.) An overview of this unbroken chain of enablement reveals the common ingredient of anointing as the source of all skills and characteristics needed for leadership. That this is the divine method is unmistakable. This anointing is God's grace working in ministry. He chooses, enables, directs, anoints. The outgrowth is effective leadership and the accomplishment of divine purpose.

As in other dispensations, the Dispensation of Law opened with bright opportunity. Israel was miraculously delivered from Egypt's bondage by God's power and experience divine providence, which kept, guided, and provided for them. They experienced unique and supernatural displays of His power, which reinforced their special place in God's plan. The record of these experiences is found in the Old Testament books of Exodus, Leviticus, Numbers, and Deuteronomy. The remainder of the Old Testament records the entering into and development and growth of Israel once in the Promised Land.

With supernatural intervention, Israel journeyed from bondage in Egypt to Mt. Sinai. Here God formed them into a nation by giving them laws, government, and social order. They are given promises, provision, and revelation of their purpose. Also they were assured by God that He would be with them. God, at Sinai, provides them with a detailed "blueprint" (or set of guidelines), which, if followed, would bring the blessings and favor of God upon their lives.

It is important to reiterate that God's plan was to use Israel as the fount of revelation to other nations concerning the glorious nature of God. God intended to manifest Himself to the nations of the world *through* Israel, and bring His blessings upon all. He permanently placed Himself in their midst in a fixed place of worship— the Tabernacle (Ex. 35.) From there He intended to administrate His government of the world through this chosen nation. God's method for doing this was to abundantly bless His people. This, in turn, would empower them to proclaim and display God's goodness to the world (Ps. 67.)

The Dispensation of Law began in the book of Exodus and continued completely through the remainder of the Old Testament finding its close in the death, burial, and resurrection of Christ.

- Exodus chapter 1 through 12:36 is the account of the early life of Moses and Israel's bondage in Egypt.

- Exodus 12:37 through chapter 18 is the account of Israel's deliverance from Egypt.
- Exodus chapter 19 through chapter 40 contains the record of Israel at Mt. SinaI where they became a nation with laws and codes (i.e., self-governing.) Here God also gave them the Tabernacle with all its attendant details for worship.
- The book of Leviticus was basically written to the Levites to instruct them regarding the proper ministry of the Tabernacle. The tribe of LevI was given no inheritance of land in the Promised Land. They were instructed by God to subsist on the income of the Tabernacle, which was provided by the tithe and offerings of the other eleven tribes. They were to be responsible for worship and for the upkeep, finances, and administration of the Tabernacle (I Cor. 9:13-14.) Striking comparisons can be made between the book of Leviticus in the Old Testament and the book of Hebrews in the New Testament.
- The book of Numbers continues the story of the nation of Israel one month after the close of the last chapter of Exodus (Ex. 40:2; Num. 1:1.) Numbers covers 39 years of wandering from SinaI to Kadesh-barnea on the east side of the Jordan River, just across from Jericho and the Promised Land.
- "Deuteronomy," the final book of the Pentateuch ("penta" = five), means "Second Lawgiving" (Gk. Septuagint.) It contains Moses' addresses to the nation during the final months of his life, at which time the children of Israel were encamped on the plains of Moab before crossing Jordan into the Promised Land. This group was not yet born when God delivered their fathers through the Red Sea, nor were they at SinaI when the Law was given. Deuteronomy can be viewed as the official history of Israel's trek from Egypt and the constitution for the nation once they were in the Promised Land.
- The book of Joshua records Israel's conquest of Canaan, the Promised Land. The books of Judges and I Samuel (through chapter 7) record the early forms of government

of the nation in which Judges loosely ruled the nation in theocratic fashion.

- I Samuel (chapter 8 to the end of the book), II Samuel, I and II Kings, and I and II Chronicles should all be read together. After requesting a monarchy (I Samuel 8:6), Israel's first king was Saul. He was succeeded by David and then by Solomon, all of whom reigned 40 years each. Under their fourth king, Rehoboam, the nation split with two tribes being called "Judah" and the other ten tribes known as "Israel" (I Kings 12.) Israel and Judah were then ruled by a succession of kings until Israel was overtaken by Assyria and Judah was overtaken by Babylon (II Kings 17:5-6; 24:1-2.)
- The books of Ezra and Nehemiah record the return of Judah (that is, the remnant of the two tribes Judah and Benjamin) to Palestine from the Babylonian captivity.
- The book of Esther records incidents that occurred while in captivity under the reign of Xerxes I, before the second expedition under Ezra and Nehemiah.
- The books of Job through the Song of Solomon are books of poetry. All of these books except Job were written during the time of the kings.
- The books of Isaiah through MalachI contain the recorded utterances of Israel's and Judah's writing prophets. Some of these prophets prophesied before the nation went into exile (i.e., Pre-exilic), some prophesied during the Exile (i.e., Exilic), and some prophesied after the return to the Promised Land (i.e., Post-exilic.) Some prophesied to Judah and some to Israel and some to both.

Malachi was the last prophet of the Old Testament and, with the close of his book, the Old Testament closes. The ensuing period of time from the end of the Old Testament to the beginning of the New Testament is often referred to as the "400 Silent Years." This was a 400-year period in which there was no prophet, and the voice of God to his people, Israel, was not heard.

TYPES AND SHADOWS

The Dispensation of Law is characterized by the use of many "types and shadows," which foreshadow biblical events that take place later. Much can be said about "types," for they are very important. While types can be found in every dispensation, the Dispensation of Law has scores of examples of such. Understanding types is essential to understanding the Bible. Following is a list of nine important points concerning types:

1. A scriptural "type" is a divinely foreordained representation of the relationship that particular persons, events, and divine institutions of the Old Testament have in relationship to corresponding persons, events, and divine institutions in the New Testament. Scripture is filled with scores of types that exemplify this phenomenon. In fact, one of the "proofs" of inspiration of the Scriptures are the many examples of foreshadowing and shades of double application between Old Testament events and their New Testament counterparts. Some examples of types follow (many more could be cited):

   a. Melchizedek was a type of Christ. (Heb. 7:1-11)

   b. Adam was a type of Christ. (Rom. 5:12-21)

   c. The Tabernacle and the Old Testament priesthood is fulfilled in the work of Christ. (Heb. 5)

   d. The Israelites going through the Red Sea is a type of Christian baptism which seals deliverance from bondage. (I Cor. 10:1-4, 11)

   e. In the Tabernacle, the veil was a type of Christ's flesh which veils the Shekinah.

   f. The Old Testament Tabernacle plan is a collection of related types that foreshadow Christ and individual salvation.

   g. O.T. Israel is a type of the N.T. Church.

   h. David is a type of Christ.

   i. The Old Testament Sabbath is a type of New Testament rest which comes by the infilling of the Holy Spirit.

2. Every type has a fulfillment or "anti-type." This "anti-type"

must have points of resemblance with the type.

3. It should be remembered that, while the type has its fulfillment, it also has its own local, original meaning that is, in many cases, separate from the anti-type.

4. While many Old Testament happenings have resemblances with later New Testament happenings, to be a true type, scripture itself interprets them as a true type.

5. A type must pre-figure an anti-type (one anti-type cannot be "typed" with another anti-type.)

6. A doctrine cannot be built upon a type, for the type is but a foreshadowing of the real fulfillment (Heb. 8:5-6; 10:1.) A type may be used only as supporting evidence to establish a particular doctrine.

7. The only points of Old Testament types that are to be applied to New Testament anti-types are those which resemble the anti-types. Other points of the type should be left alone, remembering that the type has its own meaning also, which is apart from the anti-type. For example, Christ on a specific occasion uses Solomon as a type of Himself. Obviously not all of Solomon's life was a type of Christ, but only that part which Christ identified (i.e., Solomon's wisdom.)

8. Both the type and the anti-type must agree with each other and with all other Scriptures on the subject of the type. A valid type never destroys the historical sense of a Scripture or the literal meaning of the words of either the type or the anti-type.

9. The anti-type, or the fulfillment of the type, is always greater than the type.

The giving of the law in the Dispensation of Law was for the purpose of providing men with an expanded basis for the knowledge of sin (Rom. 3:19-20; 4:15; 5:13, 20.) Mankind already had knowledge of sin. However, with the coming of the Law, the knowledge of what was correct or incorrect was greatly expanded. As such, the law acted as a "schoolmaster" (Gal. 3:24-25) and the whole of the law itself was a "type" (or "shadow") of "good things to come" (Heb. 10:1.)

The Dispensation of Law ended in failure—culminating in Israel's refusal to accept the Messiah and their guilt in crucifying Him. The chosen people, through whom God brought the Messiah, collaborated in His crucifixion. *"He came unto his own, and his own received him not"* (Jn. 1:11.) They did not exhibit faith, but rather, as in all previous dispensations, rebellion and unbelief ruled the day.

With the coming of Christ, the law and its demands were fulfilled (Mt. 5:17-18), for the law "was" until John (Lk. 16:16.) *"Christ is the end of the law for righteousness to everyone that believeth."* The Old Covenant of the law was "abolished" and "done away" (II Cor. 3:6-18.)

This dispensation ended with God making provision for redemption through Calvary, the resurrection, and the infilling of the Holy Spirit. Christ met the demands of the law for all, and made redemption available to all who believe (Jn. 3:16.) When Christ is received in one's life through the infilling of His Spirit, grace is provided to live above the condemnation of the law. Liberty from sin's hold is provided once and for all—and remains effective as the believer walks in the Spirit (Rom. 8:1.)

THE TIMES OF THE GENTILES

In this dispensation of the Law, a new phrase is encountered called "the times of the Gentiles" (Lk. 21:24.) Later the phrase "fullness of the Gentiles" (Rom. 11:25) will also be encountered. While somewhat similar sounding, it is evident that they are not the same thing. The "fullness of the Gentiles" appears to be equivalent to the church age. In contrast, the "times of the Gentiles" began when Israel, as a nation, first became subject to Gentile empires. This occurred long after they had become a nation at Sinai. This took place in 606 B.C. when Judah became subject to Babylon. The Northern Kingdom had preceded Judah into captivity to Assyria more than a century before Judah becomes subject to Babylon. With the fall of Judah, which was the Southern Kingdom, now the entire nation was in subjection to Gentile powers. It will remain so until Christ returns and reestablishes Israel's independence once and for all (Rev. 19:1.)

While Israel presently is enjoying its first official freedom from Gentile domination (gained in May 1948) in some 2500 years, it is, nevertheless, not independently the "head" and not the "tail" (Deut. 28:13), which is promised by God. Israel remains dependent on the Gentiles (e.g., the United States and others.) It will only be the true leader of all nations and close the "times of the Gentiles" when Christ returns at the Second Coming and is accepted by them as their true Messiah. Until then, they will remain under Gentile domination. This period of their domination is defined as the "times of The Gentiles."

The significance of Israel's independence in 1948 should not be overlooked. This event reflects the beginnings of a fulfillment of Matthew 24:32-35, the fig tree being Israel and the budding being their re-emergence from the long winter of "desolations" (Dan. 9:26), which they experience during the times of the Gentiles.

It is also important to keep in mind that the nation of Israel in the Old Testament, while sharing with the Church many spiritual fulfillments of prophecy, is, nevertheless, not the church in the New Testament—even though Israel is spoken of as *the church in the wilderness*" (Acts 7:38.) The word "church" is translated from the Greek word "ekklesia," which means "the called out ones." Israel is God's Old Testament "called out ones," just as the New Testament church is the "called out ones" in the present time.

Israel was called out of all nations to fulfill the purpose of God. God's purpose for Israel was as follows:

1. To be the fount of God's blessings to the other nations of the earth (Gen. 12:1-3; Mt. 21:33-46; Rom. 9:4-5; 11:25-29.)
2. To be true to the one "true God." In doing so, they would be a distinct, holy, separated people (Gen. 12:1-3; Ex. 19:5-6.)
3. To bring the Savior into the world (Gen. 3:15; Isa. 9:6; Micah 5:2) to be the head of all nations on earth during the Millennium, at which time Christ shall rule the Earth—both during the Millennium and forever after (Deut. 28:13; Isa. 9:6-7; Dan. 7:13-14; Rom. 11:29.)

Israel is God's earthly people and clearly has earthly (as well as spiritual) promises. Israel was governed by earthly laws, and was promised an everlasting possession of the actual real estate of the land of Promise. While the Gentiles in the present Church Age are recipients of the spiritual promises made to Israel (e.g., Joel 2:28-29; Acts 2:15-21; Gal. 3:7, 9, 14, 29), they are not recipients of the promises of an earthly inheritance nor is the church God's earthly people (Heb. 12:22-24.) These earthly promises to Israel are so explicit, so numerous, and so emphatic that they can hardly be overlooked or allegorized.

The apostle declares that Israel is presently in a state of spiritual "blindness in part" (Rom. 11:25), a state in which they will remain until the Church Age, or the "fullness of the Gentiles," is completed. This does not mean that individual Jews cannot be (or are not) saved during the Church Age, for they are. As a nation, however, Israel still does not accept (or recognize) the Christ-Messiah and consequently still remain blinded to His work and identity in the earth. Nevertheless, scores of scriptures, reveal that God will restore the nation of Israel to the place He has chosen for them (e.g., Isa. 11:10-16; 43:1-7; Jer. 16:14-15; 30:10-24; Ezk. 11:17-21; Rom. 11.)

The time of the full restoration of the nation of Israel will bring to a close the "times of the Gentiles." The Jews will recognize Christ, accept Him, and follow Him (Mt. 23:38-39; 24:27-31; Lk. 21:24; Zech. 12:10; 14:21; Isa. 11:10-11; Acts 3:20-26.) However, just prior to their turning to Christ, Israel will go through the time of "Jacob's trouble" (or the Great Tribulation.) Having accepted, and been duped by, the Antichrist (Jn. 5:43), they will become victims of the viciousness of the Antichrist and be subjected to a time of trouble such as has never been seen (Mt. 24:5-21.) They will, however, through much sorrow, recognize their mistake and accept Jesus Christ as the Messiah. This acceptance will usher in the completeness of the Kingdom of Heaven on earth with Christ as universal Lord and King.

The Dispensation of the Church

This dispensation is called the Dispensation of the Church, or the Church Age, or Dispensation of the Spirit, or Dispensation of Grace, because of the grace of God, through the Spirit, that is being poured out on mankind in a way (and in a measure) never before experienced. *"For the law was given by Moses, but grace and truth came by Jesus Christ"* (Jn. 1:17.)

The word "grace," when used as an attribute of God, means God's "free-giving" of His unmerited love, favor, and empowerment, without regard to the worthiness of the recipient. It includes God's empowerment for the individual to live delivered from the bondage of sin. God's grace has been extended to man in all ages. The many Old Testament examples of God's blessings upon people and nations are illustrations of God's undeserved favor or grace.

However, there is another reason for using the term "Spirit" and the term "grace" in connection with this dispensation. First, the Holy Spirit is the medium through which Grace comes. The two terms, as used in the New Testament, are virtually inseparable. For example, the "gifts of the Spirit" which are listed in I Corinthians 12, are, in reality, "gifts of Grace" (Gr., *charismata*.) Grace is poured out through the Spirit upon believers (Acts 2:38, 10:46-48; 19:6, etc.)

Scripture makes a particular contrast between the Dispensation of Grace and the period that immediately precedes it, the Dispensation of Law. Repeatedly the Dispensation of Grace is depicted as being superior to the Dispensation of Law (II Cor. 3.) The Dispensation of Law demanded man's obedience, but did not empower him to so do (Rom. 7:15-25.) In contrast, grace, through the baptism of the Holy Spirit, provided the way to please God, and empowered man to do so (Rom. 8:1-5.) The law demanded justice, but could not justify. Thus, the result was death—the just penalty for sin. On the other hand, grace did not remove the demands of the law, but fulfilled those demands for death through the death of Christ. He died once and for all. Just as the curse of sin and death came by one man—Adam—so justification and life came by the "second

Adam"—Christ (I Cor. 15:45; Rom. 5:12; 15-21.) The unmerited favor of God provided Jesus Christ as the Savior who took the sins of the world upon Himself. This provided the way for God's blessing to fall upon those who believe.

Divine purpose in this dispensation, as declared by James and the first church council, is to take out of the Gentiles a people for Christ's namesake (Acts 15:14.) This dispensation does not fit in Daniel's schema of 70 weeks because the 70 weeks are determined upon Israel, not the church. Thus, he sees the Church age as a time of "desolations" upon Israel. Of the seven transitional periods we call dispensations, the Church age dispensation is the only one in which the primary action is God "calling out" a people from the Gentiles for His namesake. While Israel will be used in the future to bring Gentiles to God (Rom. 11:12, 15) Gentiles are brought to God today primarily without Jewish involvement. Again, the church is clearly not the nation Israel. The church, in this dispensation of the Spirit, does receive the spiritual blessings promised to Israel in the Old Testament (Joel 2:28-29; Acts 2:16-18.) However, it does not inherit the natural promises made to Israel regarding the land promised to Abraham. Those promises of land, national prominence, etc., remain to be fulfilled by a restored Israel (Acts 15:16-17; Rom. 11:15, 23, 25-26.) Israel, though presently blinded "in part," shall yet have the scales removed from their eyes at a future date and become the recipient of both the natural as well as the spiritual promises given to them.

God's method for accomplishing His purposes in this dispensation is the powerful proclamation of the "good news" of what He has provided through Calvary. The "good news" (or "gospel") is that Christ died in our stead, was buried, and rose again—victorious over sin, disease, and death. Peter, on the birthday of the church, revealed that this good news is applied to an individual's life through repentance (death), water baptism in the name of Jesus Christ (burial—"*we are buried with him by baptism*" Rom. 6:4), and the infilling of the Holy Spirit (resurrection—"*we shall be also in the likeness of his resurrection*" Rom. 6:5; Acts 2:38.)

The Dispensation of Grace will also end in man's general failure to grasp God's opportunity for salvation—and will result in judg-ment (which will come in the person of the Anti-Christ and in the coming of the Great Tribulation) out of which will come the Second Coming, or Revelation of Jesus Christ in which every eye shall see him at the battle of Armageddon Rev. 19:7)

This Dispensation of the Church, or Church Age, or Dispensa-tion of the Spirit, or Dispensation of Grace, or the "fullness of the Gentiles" (Rom. 11:25) is a time when God is taking out of the Gentiles "*a people for his name*" (Acts 15:14.) The Church Age is "the kingdom of God" (Rom. 14:17) in the earth, but in a way that was very obviously unexpected and not understood by the Jews of Jesus' day. Like seed planted under the ground the seed of the Word of God is planted in the hearts of men (Mt. 13:23), this in contrast to the resplendency of the physical kingdom which they were expect-ing. God's concern in the Church Age is to overthrow rebellion and condemnation in men's hearts rather than the political overthrow of the nations of the earth. In contrast, Christ will return at his second coming to set up a literal, material kingdom, not only in the hearts of men but also in political domination of all nations of the earth.

John the Baptist began his ministry with the declaration, "*Repent ye: for the kingdom of heaven is at hand*" (Mt. 3:2.) An oft-repeated question is what is the Kingdom of Heaven?

The Kingdom of Heaven, which John proclaimed to be "at hand," when fully consummated in its final form, is literally Heaven's rule on earth with King Jesus himself reigning. Hypothetically, had John's hearers accepted his message and thereby accepted the King of the Kingdom (Christ), the literal Kingdom of Heaven on earth could have become a reality at that moment. Israel, through Christ, would have ruled the world and avoided the trouble they have had and will experience. Gentiles evidently would have had the opportunity to ac-cept the King, but only under (and through) national Israel, the same opportunity which will be afforded them in the Millennium (Isa. 6.)

The question has been asked, could this have happened? The idea that God could offer humankind a real choice and opportunity, knowing all the while that humankind would fail (and, in fact, having decreed a plan on the basis of that failure) is expressed in other passages of scripture. For example, in the Garden of Eden what would have happened to Jesus and the Cross if Adam and Eve had not sinned? Did God make them sin? Obviously not. Nevertheless, he had already provided for their, and our, salvation.

At any rate, with Israel's rejection of the King, the establishment of the literal, material, earthly rule of Christ on the earth remained future (Rev. 19.) However, Paul makes clear that Israel will someday yet accept Christ as Messiah, and God will fulfill the scores of Old Testament prophecies to establish them in the earth as the head and not the tail (Deut. 28:13; Rom. 11:26.) This will be the establishment of the Kingdom of Heaven on the earth. Presently, the world is obviously not living in the literal, earthly, Kingdom of Heaven on earth. Believers are, however, living presently in the Kingdom of God, *"for the kingdom of God is not meat and drink; but righteousness, and peace, and joy in the Holy Ghost"* (Rom. 14:17.)

Below are some of the differences and similarities between the time of the complete rule of the Kingdom of Heaven on earth and the Kingdom of God on earth as we presently find it.

Some of the differences are:
- The Kingdom in the *present* is only within the hearts of individuals (Mt. 13:23.)
- The Kingdom in the *future* will be both within the hearts of men, as well as without, that is, in political dominance throughout the earth.
- The Kingdom in the *present* is spiritual but not material (Rom. 14:17)
- The Kingdom on earth in the *future* is spiritual as well as material and political (Isa. 9:7.)
- The Kingdom in the *present* is invisible (Lk. 17:20-21.)
- The Kingdom in the *future* Millennium will be both visible and invisible (Mt. 24:30, 31.)
- The message of the Kingdom in the *present* is to repent and obey the Gospel, in preparation for the catching away of the church to

the marriage supper of the Lamb (I Thes. 4:3, 7, 13-17.)

- The message in preparation for the *future* Kingdom physically on earth will be to repent and obey the Gospel, for the Lord who is judge of all is returning to the earth. (Mt. 24:42, 44)

Some similarities are:

- Entry into God's kingdom, whether *present* or *future*, will require obedience to the same Gospel and will usher all into the same spiritual kingdom. There is only one gospel message that derives directly from Christ's death, burial, and resurrection, and applied to individual lives on the Day of Pentecost. Peter's message on the birth of the church on the Day of Pentecost (Acts 2:38) was, and is, and will be, the saving message for all mankind, *present* or *future*.

- The primary rule of both *present* and *future* will be from within the individual (i.e., spiritual) by the Holy Spirit (Jer. 31:31-34; Rom. 12:17.) The kingdom in the *present* is the invisible kingdom of God's throne in men's hearts. His domain is their life. God's rule in the *future* is not only within, but is a visible, political rule.

- The guarantee of the safety and security of both *present* and *future* is grounded in Christ, who is the image of the invisible God, and by whom all things consist (Col. 1:15-18.)

- Both experience the spiritual reality of the new covenant (Jer. 31:31-34; II Cor. 3.) However, the Kingdom in the *present* (the church) is not the literal, earthly, political kingdom that the Kingdom in the *future* will be.

- The kingdom in the *future* is the completed form of the kingdom, that is, both inward and outward. The kingdom in the *present* is the kingdom in "mystery" form (Mk. 4:11), that is, only within the hearts of men. Those who are experiencing the kingdom in its *present* form are, in fact, "tasting" of the *future*, or, "world to come" (Heb. 6:4, 5.) This would be impossible if there were no "world to come." (For more on the Kingdom, see "Dispensations, The Gospel and The Kingdom", on page 106.)

The Church Age begins with the birth of the church on the Day of Pentecost, shortly after the resurrection and ascension of Jesus (Acts 2:1-4.) It will close with the catching of the church out of the earth (I Thes. 4:14-18, Rev. 4:1.)

The birth of the Church Age was predicted by Christ (Mt. 16:18.) The church (Gr. "ekklesia") is the called-out ones (Acts 15:14.) God purchased the church by the shedding of His own blood (Acts 20:28.) One becomes a part of the church by believing the Gospel (Jn. 7:37-39), and being born again (Jn. 3:5; Acts 2:38.) The church is not a man-made organization, but rather, is comprised of all who respond in faith to the Gospel message given on the birthday of the church (Acts 2:38.)

The Church Age, or Dispensation of Grace, (or, Dispensation of the Spirit) is characterized by the indiscriminate outpouring of the Spirit upon all who believe. While the Spirit rested on and in select people prior to the Day of Pentecost, it was never given to "whosoever will", and was for empowerment for service only. John makes a marked distinction between the notion of the Holy Ghost within the individual *before* the resurrection as opposed to *after* (Jn. 7:35-39.) Having the Holy Spirit on, or within one, prior to Pentecost was an empowerment for service. In contrast, receiving the Holy Spirit on the Day of Pentecost had obvious soteriological significance. As recorded in Acts 2, Peter declared, *". . . this is that which was spoken by the prophet Joel . . . I will pour out my Spirit upon all flesh . . ."* (Acts 2:16-17.) Peter further expanded, declaring, *"For the promise is unto you, and to your children, and to all that are afar off, even as many as the Lord our God shall call"* (Acts 2:39), and reveals it to be basic to salvation (Acts 11:14, 15, 17; 15:8, 9, 11.) Jesus promised the Spirit (Jn. 7:37-39; 14:16-18), "acted out" for them how it would come (Jn. 20:22), promised that it would empower them (Acts 1:8), explained that they would speak with tongues (Jn. 3:8; Mk. 16, 17) and poured it out upon them (Acts 2:1-4.)

While other dispensations made demands upon man that could not be met, the Dispensation of Grace empowers man with overcoming enablement. Salvation (as in Rom. 1:16) means "deliverance." It is a time when the Holy Spirit in man renews and regenerates him (II Cor. 5:17; I Cor. 6:9-10.) The Gospel, in human lives, delivers people from the curse and power of sin and replaces it with peace and joy (Rom. 14:17.) As one walks and lives under the glory and grace of God, divine empowerment strengthens him, preventing his falling back under the curse of sin. This does not mean that one who has been saved cannot still be lost, for there is still the possibility of backsliding (Gal. 5:4; Jude 24; Lk. 8:13; I Cor. 9:27; Heb. 2:1-3; James 5:19-20.)

The Apostolic church emphasized three things as critical to initiation into the church. These include repentance, baptism (in the name of Jesus Christ), and the infilling of the Holy Spirit. This emphasis is seen repeatedly in the early history of the church (Acts 2; 8:16, 10; 19:1-6.) Even a cursory perusal of the book of Acts reveals that it was the norm in the New Testament church for believers to receive the Holy Spirit in the same manner as happened on the day of Pentecost (Acts 2:1-4; 11:12-17; 15:8-11; I Cor. 12:13.) The baptism of the Holy Spirit was accompanied by speaking in other tongues. This was a fulfillment of Isaiah's prophecy.

> *"For with stammering lips and another tongue will he speak to this people. To whom he said, this is the rest wherewith ye may cause the weary to rest; and this is the refreshing"*
> –Isaiah. 28:11-12

This dispensation is characterized by the fact that supernatural signs accompany the preaching of the good news to humanity. Signs, wonders, divine healing, and miracles are clearly a part of the manifestation of God's power in this period (Mark 16:17-18; James 5:14-15; John 14:12-14.)

Severe spiritual darkness has challenged the church in this dispensation. Some 300 years after the apostles, spiritual apostasy and doctrinal error became rampant. For 1,000 years (from approximately 500 A.D. to 1500 A.D.), many lived in intense ignorance of God's promises and existed in spiritual darkness. Although there were those throughout history that experienced God's truth for this dispensation, significant change unfolded with the advent of the reformation in the 1500s. Light began to re-emerge, and a movement towards enlightenment and a revival of biblical Christianity gained momentum. Institutional control gave way to individual conscience. From the 16th century forward, keen interest in the Bible and the things of God propelled Luther, Calvin, Zwingli, the Wesleys, Charles Spurgeon, Charles Finney, George Whitefield, Jonathan Edwards, Francis Asbury, the Albigenses, the Waldenses, the followers of Menno, the Anabaptists, the Puritans, the Shakers, the Quakers, the Presbyterians, Methodists, Baptists, the holiness people, and many others toward a return to the dynamic life of New Testament Christianity. To varying degrees, they and others moved toward the rediscovery of crucial elements of both the truth and dynamic spiritual life of biblical Christianity. The ability to think critically did not lead away from discovery of living Christianity, but rather, directly toward it.

Out of this came a great renewal of individual transformation and revival. On New Year's Day, 1901, a group of Bible school students were praying in Topeka, Kansas, when the Holy Spirit fell upon them. They began to speak in tongues as the Spirit gave utterance. From then until the present time, a worldwide revival of New Testament experiential Christianity has swept and is sweeping the world. The Pentecostal experience of Acts 2 has crossed, and is crossing, every denominational, ethnic, and religious barrier. Close scrutiny of church history clearly shows that the true, Bible believing church has always existed since the Day of Pentecost. However, in these last days, the church is experiencing a renewed revival unmatched since the days of the apostles in which a significant portion of the world's population claims to be Pentecostal. Further, this dramatic, exponential growth shows no signs of slowing.

The Church Age will end when the "fullness of the Gentiles" is complete, when a completed number of souls are saved (Rom. 11:25.) The church is instructed to look for a dramatic ending to this dispensation. This ending is called *"that blessed hope."* We are *"looking for that blessed hope, and the glorious appearing of the great God and our Savior Jesus Christ"* (Tit. 2:13.)

THE CATCHING AWAY OF THE CHURCH

> *For the Lord himself shall descend from Heaven with a shout, with the voice of the archangel, and with the trump of God: and the dead in Christ shall rise first. Then we which are alive and remain shall be caught up together with them in the clouds to meet the Lord in the air, and so shall we ever be with the Lord*
>
> —I Thes. 4:16-17

The Church Age will end with the catching up of the church into Heaven. This will not be the end of the history of the world or of mankind living on the earth. It will, however, end the Church Age, as the church is caught up to be with the Lord. This exciting and supernatural event is simply and clearly expressed in numerous places in the New Testament such as I Thess 4:13-17; I Cor. 15:23, 51-58; John 14:1-3; Luke 21:34-36; Rev. 4:1. Special insight into obscure passages is not required for one to understand the fact of the catching away of the church. ("Catching away" is translated into Latin as "raptura" and into English as "rapture.") For example I Thess. 4:16, 17 describes this event with crystal clarity:

> *For the Lord Himself shall descend from Heaven with a shout, with the voice of the archangel, and with the trump of God: and the dead in Christ shall rise first:...Then we which are alive and remain **shall be caught up** together with them in the clouds, to meet the Lord in the air: and so shall we ever be with the Lord.*
>
> —I Thess. 4:16, 17

The catching away of the church is a purely New Testament doctrine. First revealed to Apostle Paul (I Cor. 15:51-58), Christ will come to catch His church away. The scripturally defined character-istics of this coming make it clear that the rapture is not the same event as Christ's second coming when every eye shall behold Him (Mt. 24:30.) The rapture is referred to as "the coming of the Lord" but is not referred to as the second coming of Christ. In contrast to the rapture, Christ's second coming for the battle of Armaged-don will not catch away people in the air, but rather, He will come to earth and will defeat the nations of the world and establish His literal throne in Jerusalem. This, in turn, will usher in the Millen-nium (Rev. 19:11-21.)

The rapture will bring the termination of the Church Age. With the exit of the church, the anti-god/anti-Christ forces will be re-leased to work their lawlessness as never before as the Great Tribu-lation is ushered in. Between the rapture of the church and the Second Coming of Christ will be a time of dark judgment upon the earth and this time referred to as the Great Tribulation (Mt. 24:21.) Judgment, which comes as a manifestation of judicial wrath or displeasure, is often seen in the Old Testament. However, the record is consistent in that, while God does bring judgment on wicked societies, He does not bring it indiscriminately on His people. For example, while the wicked earth was judged in Noah's day, the righ-teous were spared and lifted above it. Likewise, Sodom and Gomor-rah experienced judgment, but Lot was first removed. In similar manner, the catching away will provide the church with an escape from this dark Day of Judgment and the wrath of God (Rev. 6:17) upon the world. Paul declares:

> But ye, brethren, are not in darkness…Ye are the children
> of light, and the children of the day: we are not of the night,
> nor of darkness…For God hath not appointed us to wrath,
> but to obtain salvation by our Lord Jesus Christ.
> –I Thess. 5:3, 5, 9

Jesus addressed this same issue, explaining that there is an av-enue of escape from this particular terrible judgment that is coming upon the earth. *"Watch ye therefore, and pray always, that ye may be accounted worthy to escape all these things that shall come to pass, and to stand before the Son of man"* (Lk. 24:34-36.) He promises that, if the disciples remain, He will then come *"and receive you unto myself, that where I am there ye may be also"* (Jn. 14:2, 3.)

Paul further makes it clear that this catching away is not a strange one-time occasion, but is one of a series of "catching aways", which, beginning with Christ himself, are all carried out in God's time and order. *". . . every man in his own order: Christ the firstfruits; afterward they that are Christ's at his coming . . ."* (I Cor. 15:23.) He goes on to declare: *"We shall not all sleep, but we shall all be changed, In a moment, in the twinkling of an eye, at the last trump: for the trumpet shall sound, and the dead shall be raised incorruptible, and we shall be changed"* (I Cor. 15:51-52.) The reason for this catching away of the church is *"that he might present it to himself a glorious church, not having spot, or wrinkle, or any such thing; but that it should be holy and without blemish"* (Eph. 5:27.) Those caught away will receive a "glorious body" in exchange for our present *"vile body,"* which will be like unto His glorious or "glorified" body (Phil. 3:20, 21.)

From these and other Scriptures it is evident that those in the church will be "caught away" to be with Jesus Christ at the Marriage Supper of the Lamb. Nevertheless, they will be judged for their works while they were on earth.

> *Now if any man build upon this foundation gold, silver, precious stones, wood, hay, stubble; Every man's work shall be made manifest: for the day shall declare it, because it shall be revealed by fire; and the fire shall try every man's work of what sort it is. If any man's work abide which he hath built thereupon, he shall receive a reward. If any man's work shall be burned, he shall suffer loss: but he himself shall be saved; yet so as by fire.*
>
> *–I Cor. 3:12-15*

THE AGE OF AGES

The Millennial Dispensation

The prophet Daniel revealed that, at the time of the end, the nation of Israel would experience what Daniel identified as a "week" (i.e., each day represents one year, thus a period of seven years) of time. Jesus explained that this great trouble would come upon Israel just prior to the Second Coming of Christ (the Second Coming of Christ is also identified as the "revelation" of Christ.) It is within this time that Israel will receive the revelation that Jesus is, indeed, the Messiah. He will also be revealed as the Messiah and King of Kings to the remainder of the world. Jesus identified this seventieth week of Daniel as the Great Tribulation (Mt. 24:21.) It is also labeled the time of "Jacob's Trouble" (Jer. 30:7.) This does not mean that the Jews have had no trouble before this, but rather, that this is a time of trouble identified with Israel (not the church) and one such as has never been experienced before. It is a time of final judgment on the nation of Israel as well as all other nations who have chosen to walk in unbelief.

This time of judgment comes in numerous ways during this period, not the least of which is the introduction of the Antichrist. The Jewish nation, along with much of the world, will be deceived into thinking that he is the true Christ (Jn. 5:43.) The Antichrist will make a covenant of peace with Israel (Dan. 9:27) and will seem to have all of the answers to the problems of the Middle East. However in the middle of the covenant, he will break his promises, placing an image of himself in the temple at Jerusalem (Mt. 24:15.) This, of course, will cause the Jewish nation to realize that this is not the true Christ. The Antichrist will then turn on them with a vengeance and fury heretofore unknown and war on them for the remainder of the week (3 ½ years.) Jesus himself describes the terror that will exist during this period of time (Mt. 24:15-26.) At the end of this period, Christ will return in glory (Rev. 19), fight for Israel, and prevail decisively, ending the control of earth by enemy forces once and for all. This victory will usher in 1,000 years of peace and prosperity upon the entire earth. This one-thousand-year period is referred to as the Millennium.

The Old Testament often refers to the Millennium by the phrase "the day of the Lord." Some Old Testament prophecies include the Great Tribulation in their descriptions of the day of the Lord rather than separate from it. Others do not mention the Tribulation as being a part of the day of the Lord but rather refer only to the Millennium proper as the day of the Lord. The Tribulation closes with the battle of Armageddon. Likewise, the Millennium will begin with the close of the battle of Armageddon. In this battle, Christ will triumph over the Antichrist and the devil and all in alliance against the Messiah will be cast with Satan into prison for 1,000 years (Rev. 20:3.) Israel will then be head of all nations (Deut. 28:13.)

At the end of the 1,000 years, Satan will be loosed for a little season. He will rally the hearts of rebellious men at that time and attempt to overthrow Christ in battle one last time. He will be defeated once again. However, this time he will be cast into the Lake of Fire forever (Rev. 20:10.) Following this will be the Great White Throne judgment (Rev. 20:11-15.)

The world has long dreamed of a global "Golden Age" of peace and prosperity. Repeatedly, military and political leaders have attempted to unite the world under a single government that would usher in an enlightenment heretofore unseen. Darius, Alexander, Caesar, Charlemagne, Napoleon, Hitler—the drive in these men was to create an idealized earth under one head. Adolf Hitler envisioned a united world government that would last 1,000 years. This has been an elusive and long-sought goal. All attempts have failed. But Christ will not fail.

Christ's success in establishing the long dreamed of Millennial kingdom does not begin with political skill or military prowess. The secret of His success penetrates beyond such and goes to the heart of all power structures, that is, the spiritual. In conquering death through His resurrection, Christ attacked the very core of all that is evil, all that ails man, the earth, its environs, and the universe itself. In doing so, He affected a deliverance that reverberates from the smallest particle of matter to the entire cosmos.

There are many wonderful consequences of Christ's victory. He can truly declare, *"I have overcome the world"* (Jn. 16:33.) The yet-to-come consequences of Christ's victory can only be described as astounding. While total deliverance from sin has already come to the spirits of believers, which are thus glorified by salvation, the physical world has not yet been so glorified. In ways that are obscure from surface observation, the earth itself yet "groans" under the effects of judgment because of sin. Further, not only the earth, but also the whole of creation, including ourselves, groan under this oppression (Rom. 8:22, 23.) Deliverance from this burden will be realized at the Second Coming of Christ and the onset of the Millennium.

Many dramatic changes in earth-life accompany the advent of the Millennium. For example, the transformation of the earth will include a renewed ability of the earth itself to produce. Rather than one or two crops a season, the land will produce in such a way that *"the plowman shall overtake the reaper and the treader of grapes him that soweth seed: and the mountains shall drop sweet wine, and all the hills shall melt."* (Amos 9:13.) Such production will obviously include changes in weather, the seasons, and accelerated growth.

In effect, the earth will apparently again approximate the environmental conditions existing prior to the Fall of man in the Garden of Eden. Man will once more be one with God and one with his environment in a seamless way. Integration into his earth, his environment, and his universe, as well as with one another, will be complete. Animals will lose their feral nature and *"the cow and the bear shall feed; their young ones shall lie down together; and the lion shall eat straw like the ox"* (Isa. 11:7.) Poisonous insects and venomous reptiles will become harmless.

And the sucking child shall play on the hole of the asp, and the weaned child shall put his hand in the cockatrice's den. They shall not hurt nor destroy in all my holy mountain: for

*the earth shall be full of the knowledge of the Lord, as the
waters cover the sea.*

–Isa. 11:8-9

The Millennium will also be marked by a significant geographical realignment of the earth's surface, particularly in the land of
Israel itself. This realignment will begin first in devastating fashion
during the Great Tribulation. The Book of Revelation, in chapters
6-18, describes these cataclysmic events. Following these events,
Christ will appear at his second coming with his saints and a
heavenly host. *"And Enoch also, the seventh from Adam, prophesied
of these, saying, Behold, the Lord cometh with ten thousands of his
saints"* (Jude 14.) This return will result in His prevailing against the
rebellious elements of this world that are gathered at Armageddon.
Christ's victory here will be accompanied by geographical upheaval
in and around Jerusalem.

> *Behold the day of the Lord cometh, and thy spoil shall be
> divided in the midst of thee, For I will gather all nations
> against Jerusalem to battle; and the city shall be taken, and
> the houses rifled, and the women ravished . . . Then shall
> the Lord go forth, and fight against those nations as when
> he fought in the day of battle. And his feet shall stand in
> that day upon the mount of Olives, which is before Jeru-
> salem on the east, and the mount of Olives shall cleave in
> the midst thereof toward the east and toward the west, and
> there shall be a very great valley; and half of the moun-
> tain shall remove toward the north, and half of it toward
> the south. And ye shall flee . . . and the Lord my God shall
> come, and all the saints with thee.*

–Zech. 14:1-5

Along with these geographical changes, still greater ones are
foretold. Ezekiel declares that a river will come into being and
flow out of Jerusalem, connecting Jerusalem to the Mediterranean

Sea in the west and to the Dead Sea in the south. The Dead Sea
will be dead no more, but will be filled with fish (Ezek. 47:1-12,
Zech. 14:8.) The position of Jerusalem, which is already situated
in the center of the world, will thus become enhanced to a much
greater extent by the creation of this river. The earthquake, which
accompanies Christ's second coming, will evidently raise the level
of the Dead Sea in such a way that it will spill out to the south,
creating a waterway which connects to Jerusalem and onward to
the Mediterranean Sea in the north and west, and likely to the
Gulf of Aqaba in the south. This waterway will be deep enough
and wide enough to accommodate net fishing, which entails ships
and deep waters (Ezek. 47:10.) As a channel, this single river will
likely dramatically increase the prominence of Jerusalem and
Israel, possibly enabling it to be a primary shipping center for
imports and exports worldwide.

It bears repeating that the positive changes that are predicted as coming with the physical Millennium kingdom will first begin in the realm
of the Spirit. Spiritual changes to mankind are foretold, that is, mankind
turning to God and receiving salvation in a worldwide revival, is the cat-
alyst for ushering in the changes described above. Precisely as predicted
in the Old Testament, man will be filled with the Spirit of the Lord and
be governed from within (Joel 2:28-29; Isa. 28:11-12; Jer. 31:33; Ezek.
37:11-14; Acts 2:1-4; 14-21.) Scripture reveals that Christ will be universally exalted as the Lord and Savior that He is. Governance during the
Millennium will not primarily be characterized by force although a "rod
of iron" is available for lawlessness. Instead, the general populace will
possess governance from within through the infilling of the Spirit which
shall dwell in them and lead and guide them into all truth.

> But this shall be the covenant that I will make with the
> house of Israel; After those days, saith the Lord, I will put
> my law in their inward parts, and write it in their hearts;
> and will be their God, and they shall be my people. And
> they shall teach no more every man his neighbour, and
> every man his brother, saying, Know the Lord: for they

shall all know me, from the least of them unto the greatest
of them, saith the Lord; for I will forgive their iniquity and
I will remember their sin no more.

–Jer. 31:33, 34

Imagine a world with no crime and no need for locks, security systems, guard dogs, and walls. Taxes will be dramatically decreased as there will be few policemen, virtually no prisons, no prison guards, few or no hospitals and health care costs, and no national military needed for defense. Who knows what degree of stress will be removed from the necessity in our world of daily attendance to such matters? Who knows how dramatic the economic revolution will be from such radical changes?

During the Millennium, Satan will be bound. However, at the close of this 1000-year period, he will again be released for a short time. And, true to form, fallen men once more will align themselves with Satan against God. This is followed by a final decisive battle in which Satan is defeated and cast forever into the Lake of Fire. This will usher in the eternal future, which is identified in Scripture as the New Heaven and New Earth (Rev. 21, 22.)

– SECTION III –

COVENANTS

Introduction to Covenants

It has already been established that, to correctly understand Scripture, one must "rightly divide" the Word. In addition to this, Paul also instructs young preachers of the importance of "sound words," and the "form" of sound words (II Tim. 1:13.) The word Paul uses which is translated "sound" is a medical term that means general well being or health. In other words, the "sound" words of Scripture produce health. In contrast, Paul elsewhere warns that a *"word will eat as doth a canker . . ."* (II Tim. 2:17.) The word translated "canker" (Gr. *"gangreaeia"*) is also a medical term and, due to its similarity to the English word gangrene, is easily recognizable.

As noted above, Paul speaks of the "form" of sound words. The word "form" used here means structure, framework, sketch, or outline. Paul thus emphasizes that the "sound words" he references come in a structure or framework. They are not random nor simply a hodgepodge of hit-and-miss scrawling, but rather, when taken together, they produce a picture or a view—they give definition, or form. Thus, when words of Scripture are "rightly divided," they are "sound words" and reveal a structural reality that includes divine intentions and purposes. One of these structural pieces that reveal God's intent is the covenants.

There are numerous covenants in scripture between men and

men, men and women, and God and humans. When we refer herein to the "covenants", we are referring to those covenants between God and people, namely, his chosen people.

The first mention of "covenant" is between God and Noah and his family and is found in Genesis 6:18. The term is introduced without prior introduction, but in a way that appears that its meaning was an assumed reality and that it was a known term.[20] This "first reference" establishes the idea of "covenant" between God and his chosen people. A covenant was an agreement or promise between two parties, solemnly professed before witnesses and made binding by an oath expressed verbally or by some symbolic action. Three examples of these easily recognizable signs or symbols of divine covenant are the rainbow with Noah, circumcision with Abraham, and the Sabbath with Moses and Israel.

Covenant language is symbolic by nature. There are many symbols which are utilized in the biblical establishment of covenants between God and man. Beyond the three mentioned above, there are many other symbols of covenants such as, blood sacrifices, architecture of the Tabernacle, temple rituals, and priest's attire. In the New Covenant, symbolic value is attached to Water Baptism, the Lord's Supper, Men's and Women's hair, Footwashing, etc. Symbols are used as communicators of spiritual truths that defy the grasp of language alone. Symbols have dual levels of meaning, reaching into the unconscious, irrational, and non-linguistic, but are bound by the structures and realities to which they refer. All symbols possess both a primary meaning as well as a secondary and the two share a unique relationship. Without losing its own ability to signify, the primary significance points to secondary meanings that cannot be understood apart from symbolic discourse.[21] The symbolism adds a new value to an object or an activity without any prejudice whatever to its own immediate value.[22] Covenants have also been identified by writers as being of several varieties, such as "dependent, concurrent, and independent", or, "commanded, promised, or agreement" type covenants.[23] A "unilateral" covenant is a covenant made by one party with another with no stated preconditions for its fulfillment. A "mutual" covenant is one made by two parties. Thus God, makes covenants with man, but their fulfillment is dependent upon an obedient response by man.

Any covenant between God and man is predicated upon divine initiative. Further, while some covenantal promises are made without stated requirements on man's part, these conditions may not directly be stated but may be presupposed. The application of the Hebrew term for "covenant" (*berit*) to an eternally valid oath as well as to a covenant that could be broken reflects the broad conceptual range for the word.[24] "The idea that in ancient Israel the *berit* was always and only thought of as Yahweh's pledging of himself, to which human effort was required to make no kind of response…can therefore be proven to be erroneous."[25] What is commonly referred to as the "Old Testament" and the "New Testament" in our Bibles should actually be termed "Old Covenant" and "New Covenant." "Old Covenant" refers to the covenant God, at Mt. Sinai, made with his Old Testament people, that is, the nation of Israel. The "New Covenant" refers to the covenant wherein God's laws are no longer written on the tables of stone (i.e., the Ten Commandments), but rather on the "tables of your heart" (Heb. 8:8-11.) This contrast is made clear in numerous scriptural passages such as II Corinthians 3:4-18 and Galatians 4:21-31.

Interestingly, the Apostle Paul speaks of the "Covenant" as well as the "Covenants." From the "Covenants" he selects the two ("Mosaic" and "New") with the broadest range of application to represent the old and the new. In a subtler, but extremely powerful way, Jesus seems to do this same thing prior to Paul. A more intense reading of the Last Supper clearly reveals this, as we shall see later in the characteristics of the New Covenant.

There are numerous other covenants in Scripture. A biblical covenant can be defined as the declaration of one person's intention, as in a will. It is made by one party who holds the power to offer a covenant that the other party can accept or reject. Such a covenant, however, has conditions, which those who desire to receive the benefits and promises of the covenant must agree to meet. In Scripture, anytime there is a will whereby one dispenses of his goods, this can be thought of as a covenant. This is also the equivalent of a "testament." Thus the Old Testament and the New Testament of the Bible can also be thought of as the Old Covenant and the New Covenant between God and His people.

Though there are, as noted above, numerous covenants in Scripture, there are eight primary ones. Further, of these eight, four have a very direct and significant impact upon believers in the church. The eight primary covenants of Scripture are: the Edenic Covenant, the Adamic Covenant, the Noahic Covenant, the Abrahamic Covenant, the Mosaic (or Sinaitic) Covenant, the Palestinian Covenant, the Davidic Covenant, and the New Covenant. The four key ones are the Abrahamic Covenant, the Mosaic Covenant, the Davidic Covenant, and the New Covenant.

However, all of the Covenants that follow the Abrahamic are a process of enlargement and extensions of God's covenant with Abraham, the covenant in which God calls out a specific man that produces a chosen people as "His" people.

The following is a basic review of these eight covenants with added attention given to the four primary ones.

Edenic Covenant
(Genesis 1:26 – 3:24)

The Edenic Covenant was made by God with Adam and Eve in the Garden. Therein, God extended continuous communion with Himself. Man was to tend the garden (Gen. 2:15), replenish the earth (Gen. 1:28) and have responsibility (dominion) over it (Gen. 1:28; Ps. 8.) God offered fellowship with Himself and all of the benefits of continuous connectedness to the infinite universe of which man was a part, including transcending the ravages of time, the ultimate expression of which is death.

Only one condition was placed on this covenant. Though Adam and Eve could have free reign in the Garden to partake of almost all aspects thereof, they could not partake of the tree of the knowledge of good and evil. This covenant included the warning that they would surely die if they ate from the forbidden tree (Gen. 2:17.)

In the event that man should break the covenant through disobedience, he would come under the dominion of time and space and matter and become subject to the law of cause and effect. He would lose his dominion over the categories of finitude and become subject to them. That is what occurred when Adam and Eve sinned. The covenant was broken, and as a result, man's contact with the infinite was broken, his spirit died, and all other aspects of his existence became subject to death (Gen. 2:17.)

However, similar to all of the dispensations, even though man broke the covenant, God provided hope by clothing Adam and Eve through the slaying of animals and giving the skins as a covering for the expelled couple (Gen. 3:21)

Adamic Covenant
(Genesis 3:14-19)

The Adamic Covenant included both explicit statements as well as deductions, which can be made based on both God's actions as well as the actions of Adam.

The stating of this covenant by God is found in Genesis chapter 3. After the Fall and expulsion of Adam and Eve from the Garden, four curses are announced. One was on the earth. Rather than yield its fruit at optimum capacity, it would bear thistles and weeds. It would also experience a significant loss of vitality, thus increasing the difficulty of extracting from it the produce of life.

The second curse was on the woman. She henceforth would experience pain in childbirth and her desire would be to her husband. (Some take this to mean that, prior to this; the physical strength of the woman was equivalent to the man.)

Third, the man was cursed. Prior to the Fall, man's work evidently consisted of pruning, maintaining, and tending the garden. However, now a new element was injected. Because the earth was cursed with weeds, thistles, and venomous living things, man's work was increased. The animals also lost much of their fear of him to the extent that, though man was still dominant among them, they no longer followed him in docile obedience but feared man and were now feral and vicious. Some believe that communication between men and animals was also greatly diminished. Man now must live and exist by the sweat of his brow. Included are the notions of loneliness, worry, stress, fretfulness, vulnerability, and the very real possibility of failure. Life is now filled with risks and vulnerability to destruction. By breaking his covenant with God through disobedience, man has now exposed himself to an entire world of terrifying realities from which he was previously immune and from which he was completely protected and unaware.

Lastly, the serpent, too, was cursed. The simple curse placed on the serpent was that he would crawl on his belly. However, his greater curse was found in this scripture:

And I will put enmity between thee and the woman, and between thy seed and her seed; it shall bruise thy head, and thou shalt bruise his heel.

–Genesis 3:15

In this curse, a hope for mankind was included. From the woman, who was victimized by the deception of the serpent, would come the source of the eventual conqueror of the serpent. This was the first promise in the Bible of the birth of Jesus. Being as there is no such thing in natural birth as "the seed of the woman," indication is here also given of Christ's future virgin birth (Isa. 7:14; Luke 1:15; Gal. 4:4.) Further, not only would He be born of the woman, He would rise up to triumph completely over the future "seed of the serpent." From the woman would come the "Son of God," a term which was also applied to Adam. In effect, the woman would produce the "Second Man" or the "last Adam" who, in contrast to the first "Son of God" who failed, would not fail but would triumph over the serpent and his seed. Thus the Adamic covenant not only supplied an immediate framework for human survival, but also provided promise and hope for the entire human race and its universe.

Noahic Covenant
(Genesis 8:20 – 9:29)

The Noahic Covenant was made between God and Noah after the Flood. Upon disembarking from the ark, God gave instructions and promises to Noah. He promised an established natural order in the earth as well as its preservation (Gen. 8:22; 9:12, 16.) Validation and provision for human self-government is established and man is given the authority to judge and execute judgment in human affairs (9:2, 3, 5, 6.) He is also directed towards both plant and animal life as sources of food (9:3, 4.) The sign of this covenant was the rainbow, which symbolized that the earth would never again be destroyed by such a deluge (9:12-17.)

Abrahamic Covenant
(Genesis 12:1-3, 17:1-7, 22:15-18)

The three preceding covenants were made long before the remaining covenants. We do not know how far back in time the Edenic Covenant was made. Neither do we know how many years may have passed from the establishment of the Adamic Covenant. At first glance, the genealogies recorded in Genesis seem to be such that exact time frames, by use of a little math, can easily and correctly be traced all the way back to man's beginnings. However, because genealogies can sometimes be reckoned from a primary historical figure to the next primary historical figure, rather than from the direct sequence of an actual father to an actual son, there may be valid reasons for exercising caution in building hard and fast conclusions on such assumptions.

At any rate, we know that God's eternal purposes were conceived *"before the foundation of the world"* (Eph. 1:4.) Rev. 13:8 declares the Lamb slain *"from the foundation of the world."* God's purposes for redemption are obviously universal. Nevertheless, all of these universal redemptive purposes are telescoped and channeled through the Abrahamic and the Davidic covenants. The salvation of humans is not accomplished by something simply "floating" out in space and time in some amorphous, philosophical, abstract way. Instead, even though redemption was conceived before the foundation of the world, it is clearly placed on a covenant basis. Thus, the whole notion of "covenant," whether Old or New Testament, revolves around the Abrahamic and Davidic covenants.

The promises to Abraham in the Abrahamic Covenant are important to us because they reflect a marked change in the methodology whereby God continued to communicate His redemptive message to all mankind, including the present time. It reveals that, rather than continue to deal with mankind directly and as a whole, God now communicated with man through an intermediary, that is, through Abraham and his descendants. This should not be interpreted as God choosing one people and abandoning His universal intentions to bring the remainder of the world to Himself. In calling Abraham, He had not "written off" the remainder of the universe. This did not signal a change in divine intent to bring the world/universe back into communion with Himself. However, His method for accomplishing this is to call out this people, who, in turn, would consecrate themselves and bring his saving message to the remainder of the inhabitants of the universe (I Pet. 2:9; Eph. 3:10, etc.) God's goodness is plainly declared to be for "all nations" (Gen. 12:3; Psa. 67.)

God's covenant with Abraham was that God would make of him a great nation. The sign of the covenant was circumcision. (Gen. 17:1-21.) God promised that Abraham would be blessed, and those that blessed him would be blessed, and those that cursed him would be cursed. Through Abraham, all the nations of the earth would be blessed. Further, Abraham's seed would be as the stars of heaven and as the dust of the earth. He and his seed would also receive Palestine as an eternal inheritance. He would be the father of many nations and kings would be born from him. The Abrahamic Covenant would be an everlasting covenant.

"Abraham's seed" is a term used to encompass all who believe on Jesus Christ. Through Christ, we all receive the spiritual promise of Abraham (Gal. 3:7, 14, 29.) As exemplified in the use of the term "Abraham's bosom" (Luke 16:22), the implications of the Abrahamic Covenant penetrate into the infinite world of the eternity. The startling truth is that the future of the entire earth is directly attached to the Abrahamic Covenant.

God's summons of Abraham is recorded in Genesis chapter 12. Following this, the entire remainder of the Old Testament deals with Abraham's descendants, which become the nation of Israel. All of God's continued dealings with, and development of, this nation is founded in the Abrahamic Covenant.

Two dominant spiritual characteristics stand out in this covenant. These are faith and obedience. Scripture forever connects the two. Paul also makes this connection:

*"By whom we have received grace and apostleship, for **obedience to the faith** among all nations, for his name . . ."*

–Romans 1:5

Abraham acted in faith and obedience and moved as a spiritual giant through history. Forsaking home, family, and friends, boldly embraces the promises of God, thus flinging himself into a world of unseen realities which, in turn, lead him to eternal greatness.

The central point of the Abrahamic Covenant is God's promise that He will produce, through Abraham, a seed of One who would bring universal hope. Through him would come a worldwide spiritual family that would also walk in faith and obedience. Thus, the Abrahamic Covenant is the foundational one.

The Mosaic (or Sinaitic) Covenant
(Exodus 19:1-6, 24:7, 8, 34:10)

Shortly after crossing the Red Sea, the children of Israel arrived at Mt. Sinai. Some 600 years had passed since God had given Abraham his covenant. From Abraham was birthed Isaac, and from Isaac came Jacob. In turn, Jacob sired twelve sons, and from these twelve sons emerges the twelve tribes of Israel which grew into the nation of Israel. Jacob son, Joseph, was taken to Egypt where, over a period of time, he became second only to Pharaoh in authority and power. Meanwhile, a great famine was impacting Palestine. Facing famine in Palestine, Jacob, hearing there was food to be had in Egypt, sends his sons there. While there, Joseph discovered them, and through a sequence of events was reunited with them. This eventually resulted in the whole family moving to Egypt where they lived in peace.

Joseph eventually died and the children of Israel, now living in Egypt, continued to grow in number. Over time, seeing this growth, a new Pharaoh became fearful of their size and proceeded to enslave them. Consequently, they remained slaves in Egypt for some 400 years. At the end of this time Moses led them out of Egypt with a mighty hand as God unleashed powerful forces upon Egypt to effect Israel's emancipation and continued growth and development (Ex. 15:26; 23:25.) This record is found in Genesis 12-50 and the early chapters of the book of Exodus. Finally, Chapters 19 and 20 of Exodus record Israel's arrival at Mt. Sinai. It is here that God gave to Moses his covenant.

With the formation of Israel, the idea of covenant assumes a new and greatly expanded perspective. Prior to the exodus the covenant promise was to individuals. Little in the way of ritual was required of them as an outward sign of obedience to the covenant. (e.g., circumcision in Gen. 17:9-14.)[26] This now changes dramatically. The Mosaic (or Sinaitic) covenant signals a sea change from the previous narrow definition of covenant. So comprehensive is the Mosaic Covenant that it becomes, for New Testament writers, "the Law" and is used as a sort of shorthand for contrasting the whole of the Old Testament with the New.

The Mosaic Covenant, as previously noted, is based upon the Abrahamic Covenant. It is an outgrowth of and further development of it. Like the Abrahamic Covenant, it was also dependent upon faith and obedience to God's Word. Atonement for sin is now provided through God giving Moses the plan for the Tabernacle and its sacrificial system. Included also was healing of sickness and disease and miraculous displays as needed to ensure their ability to reach the Promised Land.

It was at Sinai that God gave the Ten Commandments (Ex. 20) and the remainder of the Law to Moses. Here God also revealed to Moses the "pattern" for the establishment of a Tabernacle on earth wherein God would dwell amongst His people. God's giving to Moses the plan for the Tabernacle signaled the first time that God established a permanent earthly dwelling place for Himself. This Tabernacle became the base for His covenant operations upon the earth. Within the Most Holy Place of the Tabernacle was placed the Ark of the Covenant. Within this Ark was placed the Tables of the Covenant or the Ten Commandments. Herein was proof that Israel was a covenant people, a people who had become a nation with a constitution written by God Himself. It was here that they were given an identity, without which slaves can never coalesce to become a people.

In covenant making, pledges or guarantees were given to show that the parties were acting in good faith. God's Ark was His continual witness to His guarantee of dwelling in the midst of Israel. This, of course, was a precursor to the time in which He would become Emmanuel or "Covenant-God with us." Thus, the building of the Tabernacle signified that God was a permanent dweller in the midst of Israel. He was with them, always present, which is in accordance with what He covenanted to do and be. He assured them that "I will be with you," "Ye shall be my people," and "I will be your God."

One might ask what God received from His covenant with Moses and Israel. The answer is found in Deuteronomy 32:9; Exodus 19:5-6 and Psalm 147:19, 20.

> *The Lord's portion is his people.*
> *Now therefore, if ye will obey my voice indeed, and keep my covenant, then ye shall be a peculiar treasure unto me above all people . . . And ye shall be unto me a kingdom of priests, and an holy nation.*
> *He sheweth his word unto Jacob, his statutes and his judgments unto Israel. He hath not dealt so with any any nation: and as for his judgments, they have not known them. Praise ye the Lord.*

Out of the covenant, God received a people consecrated unto Him who would commune with Him. They belonged to Him and were expected to act as ambassadors in the carrying out of His actions and intentions in the earth. The greatest thing that emerged out of the Sinaitic Covenant was the development of a people who were God's exclusive people. They were a gift to the earth through which all of the nations of the earth would be blessed.

The Palestinian Covenant
(Deuteronomy 27:1—30:20)

The Palestinian Covenant is a covenant that God made with Israel in which they were promised a "land," that is, an actual piece of real estate that would be theirs forever. Again, like all covenants, it was predicated upon obedience (Deut. 11:8-32; Lev. 26:1-46) and included the promise of dispersion from the land in the case of disobedience (Deut. 30:1; 28:63-68.) If dispersed, however, they were promised a restoration to the land contingent upon repentance while in the dispersion (Deut. 30:2; Zech. 2:10-14.)

Israel was also promised national blessing (Deut. 30:9-10; Rom. 11) and judgment upon those that oppressed them (Deut. 30:7; Zech. 14.) Also included in this covenant was a promise of the return of the Lord to establish them permanently in the land (Deut. 30:3; Rev. 19.)

Also worth noting is that Israel was and is God's *earthly* people with an earthly future and an earthly home. The church is also Abraham's children by faith (Gal. 3:7, 14, 29) but are designated a *heavenly* people (Eph. 1-3; Hebrews 12:18-28.) Throughout history, numerous groups of Christian Gentiles and even nations (e.g., "British-Israelism) have taken to themselves the identity as earthly Israel. With this, they often view their homeland as being the "true land of Israel." Numerous forms of national elitism and bigotry has resulted from this incorrect identity. This belief system is erroneous because the church is not destined to a permanent earthly home as is Israel.

> For ye are not come unto the mount that might be touched, and that burned with fire . . . and so terrible was the sight that Moses said, I exceedingly fear and quake: But ye are come unto mount Zion, and unto the city of the living God, the heavenly Jerusalem, and to an innumerable company of angels, To the general assembly and church of the firstborn, which are written in heaven, and to God the Judge of all,

and to the spirits of just men made perfect, And to Jesus the mediator of the new covenant, and to the blood of sprinkling, that speaketh better things than that of Abel.

–Hebrews 12:18, 21-24

And hath raised us up together, and made us sit together in heavenly places in Christ Jesus . . .

–Eph. 2:6

The Davidic Covenant
(II Samuel 7:1-17, I Chronicals17:11-14)
(Expanded in Psalm 89:20-37)

The Davidic Covenant included the following:

1. God would establish David's house, throne, and kingdom, forever and make Israel a sure land forever. (II Sam. 7:12-16)
2. Christ would be born from David's seed. (Acts 13:33)
3. David's seed would not see corruption (Ps. 16:10)
4. Like others, this was an eternal covenant (II Sam. 7:10-16)

The Abrahamic Covenant was continued through the Davidic. More than others, these two covenants provide the deep and broad foundation for the New Covenant. There is a special emphasis on *surety* in this covenant. In this vein, it was stated to be as sure as the movements of the heavenly planets and as certain as the seasons (Ps. 89:20-37; Jer. 33:20-26.) David, in reference to the covenant when he was dying, said that it was *"ordered in all things and sure"* (II Sam. 23:5.) Paul preached about these covenant promises. The promise was given from God stating, *"I will give you the sure mercies of David"* (Acts 13:34.)

The Davidic Covenant was unique in that here was introduced for the first time the idea of a "Tabernacle of David." Prior to this, it may have been acceptable to speak of "Moses' Tabernacle" or the "Tabernacle in the Wilderness." The Tabernacle as we find it with Moses was bloody and characterized by somberness and death. Other than the blowing of trumpets as signals, no music was included. In direct contrast to this, the Tabernacle of David was primarily characterized by celebration and joy. The Psalms, many of which David wrote, overflow with joy, dancing, praise, worship from the heart, and expressiveness. David was characterized as a "man after God's own heart." The book of Psalms became Israel's songbook. It is remarkable to sing Psalms written some 3,500 years ago and see how startlingly they apply to the human situation today. The core nature, desires, and needs of the individual remain unchanged in every age.

A repeated characteristic of the Covenant of David is that God would *"beat down his foes before his face"* (Psalm 89:23) and that his kingdom would expand into immeasurable dimensions. The power and importance of being a "covenant man" can be seen in the account of David and Goliath. While the size and bold boast of Goliath terrified the armies of Israel, David remained unfazed and derisively referred to the giant as that "uncircumcised Philistine." In contrast, David was an Israelite with the covenant sign of circumcision which was the sign, the surety, that his covenant God would not leave him alone to be defeated.

The Davidic Covenant also played a pivotal role in the book of Revelation In writing to Philadelphia, John declared:

> *And to the angel of the church in Philadelphia, write; These things saith he that is holy, he that is true, he that hath the key of David, he that openeth and no man shutteth; and shutteth, and no man openeth . . .*
>
> –Rev. 3:7

A key is a symbol of authority and power (Mt. 16:18-19.) Through Christ, God used the Davidic key to empower the church in Philadelphia.

David is also mentioned two more times in the book of Revelation. In chapter 5, John wept because there was a great book, which no man could open. The Lamb, as "the root of David," prevailed over the satanic powers that had captured the earth. Again, Revelation 22:16 reveals Christ as the eternal victor, and here He identifies Himself as *"the root and offspring of David."* Thus the Davidic Covenant is the ground for our understanding of the surety of Christ's victories both now and in the future!

The New Covenant
(Jeremiah 31:31-34, Hebrews 8:9-11)

As already noted, the word "testament" used in our Bible, as in "New Testament" and "Old Testament," can also be translated as "covenant." The birth of Jesus signaled the ending of the Old Covenant and the beginning of the New Covenant. This transition was a process of moving from the old to the new. The Old Covenant came by Moses, and the New Covenant came by Jesus Christ (Jn. 1:17; Gal. 3:19; Heb. 9:15; Mt. 26:28.) The Old Covenant was ratified by the shedding of the blood of bulls and goats, and the New Covenant was ratified by the shedding of the blood of Jesus Christ (Ex. 29:1-8; Mt. 26:28.) The Old Covenant had many sacrifices; the New Covenant had only one (Heb. 9:9-14; Heb. 10:14; Rom. 6:6-13.) The first demanded righteousness but couldn't give it while the new gave righteousness (Lk. 10:28; Rom. 8:1-4; Gal. 3:1-29; 5:1-26.) The first brought wrath, the other brought salvation from wrath (Rom. 4:15, 5:9; Gal. 3:13-14.) One was made to be changed while the other was made to be unchanged (Heb. 7:11-22; 8:5-6; 9:9-10; 10:9; 13:20.)

The outstanding event that signaled that the Old Covenant had come was the giving of the Ten Commandments written on stone (as well as the remainder of the Law) at Sinai. In contrast, the outstanding event that signified (and continues to signify in each individual heart) that the New Covenant had come was *not* the writing of God's law on tables of stone, but rather "written in our hearts." In other words, God's laws are placed within us in our hearts and in our spirits. This is what the Holy Spirit baptism is and does. It was of this that Jeremiah prophesied, saying:

Behold, the days come, saith the Lord, that I will make a new covenant with the house of Israel, and with the house of Judah Not according to the covenant that I made with their fathers in the day that I took them by the hand to bring them out of the land of Egypt; which my covenant they brake, although I was an husband unto them, saith

*the Lord; But this shall be the covenant that I will make
with the house of Israel; After those days, saith the Lord,
I will put my law in their inward parts, and write it in their
hearts; and will be their God, and they shall be my people.
And they shall teach no more every man his neighbor, and
every man his brother, saying, saying, know the Lord; for
they shall all know me, from the least of them unto the
greatest of them, saith the Lord; for I will forgive their iniquity, and I will remember their sin no more.*

–Jer. 31:31-34

As we have already noted, the Apostle Paul speaks of the "Covenant" as well as the "Covenants." From the "Covenants" he selects
the two ("Mosaic" and "New") with the broadest range of application to represent the old and the new. In a subtler, but extremely
powerful way, Jesus seems to do this same thing before does Paul.
A close reading of the Last Supper clearly reveals this interesting
combination of action and discourse by Jesus.

Both Matthew and Mark's account of the last supper record
Jesus as saying "This is my blood for the covenant which is poured
out for many." In contrast, both Paul and Luke say, "This cup is
the new covenant in my blood." Only Luke and Paul mention "the
New Covenant" but only Matthew and Mark mention that it is
"for many." All of this is carefully written to bring to the surface
total spectrum of the core Old Testament Covenant ideas. Thus,
the reference to the cup from Matthew and Mark is a direct de-
rivative of the Sinaitic covenant in which the blood is sprinkled,
by Moses, first on God (that is, on the altar, which represents the
hidden God), and then on the people, saying "Behold the blood
of the covenant which the Lord has made with you in accordance
with all these words" (Ex. 24:8.)[27] The idea here was, as it is with
the entire Old Testament system of blood sacrifices, that making
a covenant was done by connecting the parties (the "many") with
a blood oath which made the alienated party a covenant part-
ner in the initiator's community. In effect, as shown by Luke and

Paul, this symbolically makes the partners to the covenant "blood brothers", that is, of the same flesh and blood. Thus, we can now see that covenant is certainly not simply about "law", but about relationship. The ritualistic Sinaitic blood sacrifice was symbolic that God now belonged to them and they belonged to God—were in fact joined by commonly held blood. In this light the oft-repeated three part formula found in both the Old Testament and New Testament takes on new meaning: "I will be your God, You shall be my people, and I shall dwell in your midst." Paul portrays this blood relationship with Christ in startling fashion exclaiming: *What? Know ye not that he which is joined to an harlot is one body? For two, saith, he, shall be one flesh. But he that is joined unto the Lord is one spirit*" (I Cor. 6:16-17.)

Jesus thus saw the Last Supper as introducing a new covenant. It is the Sinaitic Covenant come to its fulfillment. Rather than destroy the old covenant, it fulfills it and expands its munificent blessings beyond Israel and to all mankind. Jesus thus becomes not only the Messiah to Israel, but also the single human whose blood is not only Jewish blood, but also human blood, creating a relational brotherhood with all peoples who will accept his offer. This is the God of the Old Testament fulfilling his purposes to bring the entirety of the universe into himself. Jesus is that God incarnated and his blood is the blood of God shed for all (Acts 20:28.) Thus when Jesus says, (as recorded by Luke and Paul) that this "cup is the new covenant in my blood" he is referencing the New Covenant announced by Jeremiah (31:31-34.) While typified by the Lord's Supper, the new covenant is not one written on stone but on the fleshy tables of the heart. It is inside, i.e, spiritual (Jer. 31:31-33; Acts 2:1-4, 38, 39.) That this is referencing the pentecostal infilling of the Holy Spirit is obvious. This explosive baptism of the Spirit on the day of Pentecost, (Acts 2) accompanied by fire and "voices" (as at Sinai) is clearly the initiation point of the New Covenant.

Scripture passages such as John 14:16-18, 26 and 15:26 show that Jeremiah's promise is fulfilled through the entrance of the Holy Spirit into the believer's life. John records further validation of this:

And when he had said this, he breathed on them, and saith unto them, Receive ye the Holy Ghost.

–John 20:22

The Greek word for "breath," "wind," and "spirit" is *pneuma*. Thus, when Jesus "breathed" on them, He was prophetically using His own breath to illustrate to them that the Holy Spirit, which they were going to receive, was literally the breath, or Spirit of God, entering into them. Is it an accident that this causes our minds to reference Adam as God *"breathed into his nostrils the breath of life; and man became a living soul"* (Gen. 2:7.) The intent was to reveal that the Holy Spirit being breathed into men's spirits was a return to life, a revival of the inward man, just as God's original breathing into man brought initial life to his soul. The first breath is into man's nostrils; the second is into his spirit and heart. Thus it is not a surprise to find that when the Holy Spirit did indeed come, it came as "breath" or "wind."

And when the day of Pentecost was fully come, they were all with one accord in one place. And suddenly there came a sound from heaven as of a rushing mighty wind, and it filled all the house where they were sitting. And they were all filled with the Holy Ghost, and began to speak with other tongues as the Spirit gave them utterance.

–Acts 2:1-2, 4

It is no accident that the longest single New Testament quotation of the Old Testament is a quote of Jeremiah 31:31-34 (See Heb. 8:9-11.)

While the coming of the Holy Spirit into the life of the believer is certainly a key component of initiation into salvation (Acts 2:38; 11:14), it is also more. The indwelling Spirit then continues to teach, lead, guide, and fulfill the role which human government, law, and culture previously fulfilled (Jn. 14:26; 15:26; Titus 2:12.) This does not mean that the one who has received this indwelling no longer has mentors, pastors, and teachers, but it does mean that the Holy Spirit not only restrains from evil but also transforms the will to a desire for righteousness. Police are not needed to ensure that the believer does right. The Spirit indwells and governs the believer from within the heart, thus revealing good and evil from the inside out, *subjectively*. In contrast, the unbeliever follows the law *objectively,* that is, as something outside of oneself.

Receiving the Holy Spirit is also equated to "entering into God's rest" (Heb. 4:4-5.) Of this, Isaiah declared:

> *For with stammering lips and another tongue will he speak to this people. To whom he said, This is the rest wherewith ye may cause the weary to rest; and this is the refreshing: yet they would not hear.*
>
> –Isaiah 28:11-12

Apostle Paul validates that the above passage from Isaiah was, indeed, referencing speaking in other tongues, thus, entering into God's rest (I Cor. 14:21.)

Also, the fourth of the Ten Commandments was to keep the Sabbath holy. The day was God's day, to be dedicated to Him by resting from all work and creative activity. The idea of "rest" on the seventh day was originally connected to the seventh day of creation in which God "rested" from creating (Heb. 6:4.) In addition, it was later connected to Israel's deliverance from Egypt in which they found "rest" from the oppression of Egypt (Deut. 5:15.) While all of the other Ten Commandments are found in the New Testament, the fourth is not. This does not mean that it was ignored, but rather, that the believer has entered into God's rest through the infilling of the Spirit (Heb. 4:9-11.) For those filled with the Spirit the Sabbath is more than simply a day or the week. They possess the "rest" within themselves and thus rest in that they are delivered from sin (as Israel was from Egypt) and also rest in the new creation of themselves resulting from God's creative work by the Spirit within their hearts and minds (Heb. 8:10; Rom. 12:2; II Cor. 5:17.)

There are many other scriptures that reveal that this spiritual rest will come to Israel.

The New Covenant which the church received at Pentecost and enjoys is actually the New Covenant promise given by God to Israel. This can be seen by the many Old Testament promises of the infilling of the Spirit which God promised Israel. While this is discussed in greater depth a little later, the fact remains that the church has received this experience, but that does nothing to negate the promises of God to Israel. Just as God repeatedly promised, life in the millennium will be characterized by this indwelling in individual Israelis and their converts.

– SECTION IV –

DISCUSSION OF DISPENSATIONS

Many aspects of biblical interpretation depend upon an understanding of dispensational and covenantal teaching. Consequently, like any major Bible subject, virtually every conceivable idea has been used against it at one time or another. Below are discussions about issues related to these important subjects.

Dispensations And Hermeneutics

We have already discussed the fact that there are a variety of ways in which the Bible self-divides. There are first the two testaments. This, of course is, in itself, a simple division. The 66 books are also obvious divisions. As previously discussed, these books, in turn, can be clumped into groups according to their content (Pentateuch, history, gospels, epistles, etc.) A case can also be made for thematic grouping by tracing a particular theme or subject thread through book after book. These groupings, and others, are, of course, extremely helpful. In addition, there are groupings of books that are of a particular genre, such as poetical books, apocalyptic books and so forth.

There are two basic methods whereby connections of particular books are ascertained. Some are obvious by simply reading the book and, through analysis, noting similarities as one breaks down the content of the book.

Once this is done of individual books, and their distinctive content is generally understood, books can also be viewed together and by *synthesis* (viewing the entirety as a unit) discover further truths which open entirely levels of understanding.

The conclusions one draws in regards to what one reads depends, to a great extent, upon the "hermeneutic" used, that is, the rules for interpreting scripture. While this is not a book on hermeneutics, nor is the intent to provide a history of biblical interpretation, a brief discussion of the hermeneutic used is appropriate in this discussion.

In reading of the early church and their response to scriptural writings, it is clear that they saw these writings as speaking plainly and literally to them. While the scripture may use different literary forms such as figures of speech, parables, and so forth, they understood that the scripture was conveying plain, understandable truths, and would self-interpret itself where needed.

However, following the apostolic age this interpretive method shifted. From approximately 400 A.D. to 1500 A.D., the general interpretive hermeneutic for the scores of old testament scriptures that predicted the future restoration of the nation of Israel became primarily *allegorical* as opposed to *literal*, or *plain*. A primary example of this is that both Catholic theology and mainline protestant theology generally taught that all the kingdom promises, and even the great Davidic covenant itself, are completely fulfilled in and through the Church." In other words, even though the many Old Testament promises which guarantee a restoration of Israel are explicit and unmistakably clear, according to this interpretive method, these scriptures do not literally mean what they say, but are allegorical in nature.[28]

The consequences of such teaching are far-reaching, including the conclusion that there is no coming Millennium, no literal second coming of Christ, no rapture, no restoration of national Israel, and no literal fulfillment of the scores of explicit Old Testament promises to national Israel. According to this allegorical method of teaching, none of these were meant by God to be taken as promises which would literally be experienced by the nation of Israel, but were God "speaking of one thing under the guise of another" (Webster, def. of "allegory.") The idea is that the allegory is an extended metaphor that, though saying one thing, it is teaching some deeper spiritual truth. Can this be correct?

It is, indeed, true that such a linguistic device may take the meaning of a plain statement beyond the author's obvious original intent. But it is untrue that an allegory eradicates the original intent of the plain statement. In the case of the plain scriptural statements regarding Israel's restoration, this allegorical method of interpretation is that God did, indeed, make these promises to a literal national people, but he actually had a deeper meaning underlying the literal meaning and the literal meaning had no meaning at all. Hence, the literal meaning has no fulfillment of its own but was simply a sort of scaffolding utilized to allegorically speak of the Church Age. The problem with such random, selective, allegorizing is that it has no boundaries. The question becomes, if these scriptures should be allegorized into meaning something they are not saying, and not meaning what they are saying, then who is to say that any other scripture should not be allegorized into a meaning other than the obvious meaning which the author intended when he chose the language which he used? As we have seen with the subject of "types", as well as in interpretation of prophetic passages, this allegorical method of interpretation brings with it serious hermeneutical problems. To assume that a scripture is "speaking of one thing under the guise of another" leaves the door to arbitrary interpretation ajar and opportunity for all kinds of fanciful and fantastic interpretations (which, history reveals, is precisely what has repeatedly happened.) A scriptural type, metaphor, or allegory, arises out of a *real, local, concrete* situation that provides interpretation to the broader, distant prophetic meaning carried in its message, but does so *without losing its immediate context and meaning.*

No text says something it doesn't mean so as to say something it does mean. An example of this is the overtly messianic Psalms (2, 22, etc.) which are, as the New Testament affirms, unquestionably speaking of Christ. However, these Psalms were written by an inspired, real man, who was writing them for, and of, himself and his time and immediate event. Though the greater meaning was of Christ, the situation out of which they were birthed was. Likewise, it is true that there are many spiritually and figuratively typological applications for today of the scores of Old Testament promises made to the nation of Israel regarding a future promised land, a land of plenty, dominion, and so forth. It is perfectly legitimate and correct to use these spiritual and figurative applications whenever and wherever needed. Nevertheless, none of this negates the fact that these scriptures still have a true local and geographical future fulfillment.

Another example is Isaiah 63 in which the Jehovah-Christ comes bloodstained but triumphant from battle, from Bozrah, the capital of Edom. The picture is one of the Lord triumphing completely over Edom, the ancient, historic, and implacable foe of Israel. The Old Testament is filled with many and varied predictions of judgment on national Edom because of their never ceasing hatred for, and opposition to, Israel. That the judgments prophesied on the real nation of Edom literally came true is now an unquestionable fact of history. Nevertheless, the greater, distant meaning of this prophecy was foretelling the coming of the Lord in a judgment on sin itself. These national and facts form a historic reality which point towards a future cosmic triumph of Christ (at Calvary) in defeating the implacable foes of God's will for the human race. This, however, did not change the actual reality of the national judgment on the literal Edom. Said prophecy was not allegorical in regards to national Edom, but actual. It was real in regards to both Edom's national demise, as well as the broader meaning of Satan's universal demise. In the same manner it is a flawed hermeneutic that identifies the messianic promises to Israel as allegorical as to Israel's national future, but "real" when applied to the church.

Although there were always those who did not follow the institutional lead of the Catholic church, the allegorical method of interpretation generally held sway until the time of the Reformation. With the Reformation this changed.

It is common knowledge that Martin Luther's historic proclamation, "the just shall live by faith" signaled an epoch reformation in curbing the power and abuses of institutional religion. However another, equally important result which was triggered was an important shift in the primary method of biblical interpretation. By placing the power of the Word as the highest authority in an individual's life, Luther began a restoration of both the primacy of the Word as well as the primacy of the individual, over the institution. The Word was given a new level of real, literal, personal meaning individually, as opposed to its contents being allegorized and institutionally mediated. Luther's proclamation signaled a return of the Word as the supreme arbiter of thought and conduct. A torrent of pent-up thirst was unleashed for the liberating, enlightening power of the plain words of the Bible for the individual. A powerful desire for a fully restored, apostolic Christianity broke forth like an uncontrollable torrent. Once unleashed, this voracious hunger for the plain Word of God changed, and continues to change, the world.

The power of this literal application of the Biblical message to individuals is revealed in subsequent history. In such an atmosphere, the definition of "Christian" was upended. The previous power of institutional control was broken. (i.e., the stranglehold of the Catholic Church on the individual.) Expanded doctrinal understanding emerged providing new insight into individual salvation, grace, water baptism, individuals receiving the Holy Spirit, and such like.

Thus not only was institutional power broken, but a hermeneutical stranglehold was also broken. A biblical interpretation emerged which emphasized, the *literal, normal, plain* meaning of scripture. These believers discovered that before a scripture takes on any expanded, figurative, symbolic, or other meaning, it first means what it says in its own place and time. While a text may be addressed to a particular person, place, or thing it can also have an expanded meaning in which that particular person, place, or thing becomes a symbol of something greater. However, these broadened meanings do not negate the local meaning.

This hermeneutical revolution played a major role in capsizing previously accepted *allegorical* methods of interpretation that often left meanings completely divorced from actual statements. These "interpreted" meanings of such passages were often determined at the arbitrary whim of whomever was doing the interpreting. Thus amillennialists, ("no millennium") including most Reformed theology, John Calvin, other pretereists, etc., must spiritualize or allegorize all Old Testament prophecies concerning Israel. Again, they do this by insisting that the Church replaces Israel and that Israel as God's chosen people has ceased to exist as such. Every Old Testament prophecy concerning the Millennium is thus something that must be spiritualized or allegorized. For example, there are many Old Testament prophecies to Israel that are clearly identified as "everlasting" (e.g., Ez. 37:26-28.) Not only do the words used indicate this, but also the contexts of such obviously mean everlasting. This of course, is problematic for the amillennialist who believes that Israel is done away and all of these specific, nationalistic, promises are somehow voided. Adam Clark's way of dealing with this was to spend considerable time articulating how "everlasting" doesn't really mean "everlasting", etc. Others negate the force of these promises by simply declaring them void. For example, W.E. Cox states: "To implement his plans God arbitrarily chose Israel to be his peculiar people only until the first advent of Christ (Gen. 49:10) By the time the church was established at Pentecost, all these national promises had been either literally fulfilled or invalidated through unbelief and disobedience."[29] The fact that Mr. Cox declares this to be so obviously does not make it so.

In summary, when discussing interpretation the terms *literal, normal,* or *plain,* mean that the first meaning of any text should be taken to mean just what it says. The text may be a straightforward statement, or a figurative statement, or a metaphor or simile, etc. Bible writers utilized a wide variety of literary devices in an attempt to convey their message as clearly and certainly as possible. We have also seen that a text that is prophetic may have an immediate meaning while also having a future meaning. The historical local event may act as a precursor, a sort of hint, or even "pre-fillment" which gestures toward the expanded meaning of that which is to come. Thus a text addressed to a particular person, place, or thing can also have an expanded meaning in which the immediate person, place, or thing becomes a symbol of something greater. For example, "Jerusalem" (Gal. 4:26), "Seed of Abraham" (Gal. 3:29), "Sion" (I Pet. 2:6; Heb. 12:22; Rom. 9:33) 'Babylon" (Rev. 17, 18), "the Sabbath" (Isa. 28:11-12; Heb. 4:1-11), "muzzle not the ox" (I Cor. 9:9-10), all have specific Old Testament meanings but also point toward future and/or eternal realities beyond their immediate meaning. However, none of this negates original meanings unique to the original time and place for which they were written, whether predictive or immediate.

Dispensations, The Gospel, and The Kingdom

One of the greatest hopes of ancient Israel was a restoration of their nation. Having been under Gentile dominion for over four centuries, it is no wonder that a great stir accompanied the coming of John the Baptist preaching "repent", for the "kingdom of heaven is at hand" (Mt. 3:1, 2.) John introduces Jesus, who in turn, also declares, "The time is fulfilled, and the kingdom of God is at hand; repent ye, and believe the gospel" (Mk. 1:15.)

There has been much discussion in regards to the hypothetical question, "Would the kingdom of God have actually come immediately had the people accepted Jesus when he was presented to them by John the Baptist?" Indeed, the question is hypothetical now, but was it then? Had they embraced Jesus and submitted to his kingship and lordship, would the millennium have begun? All answers are, of course, hypothetical also, because they did not accept him, and consequently the question becomes moot. If pressed to respond, the correct answer seems to be "yes", they could have accepted him, and "yes", had they done so, the kingdom would have immediately been ushered in upon earth. He knew, however, that they were not going to accept him as numerous prophecies revealed this. Nevertheless, it does not automatically follow that, because of prophecy, they had no alternative except to reject him. Knowing what man will do, and causing him to do it, is not the same thing.

On the other hand, without Christ's shed blood on Calvary, the redemption of the race could not be accomplished. Further, the New Testament reveals that Christ was slain "from the foundation of the world", indicating that it was obvious and unavoidable that it should be so. How could there be a kingdom where sin has been conquered without Calvary? The obvious answer is, there could not.

At any rate, the kingdom was announced and was apparently in the realm of possibility of coming physically with Jesus as the corporeal, physical king. However, it did not, this in spite of the fact that the people fully expected that with the advent of the Messiah would also come his immediate introduction of the physical kingdom with himself as King. Instead, Jesus taught them that the kingdom, at least for this time, would come in "hidden" fashion. As recorded in Matthew, chapter 13, he is emphatic regarding this, going into extensive detail to make this clear.

In this chapter Jesus cites seven different examples of the Kingdom in which all of them share a pronounced, common characteristic. This common trait is that the kingdom at this time is characterized by "hiddenness." Seed sown, wheat and tares sown, mustard seed sown, leaven hidden in a loaf, treasure hid in a field, pearl hidden in an oyster, or a fishing net cast into the sea—the constant in all is that the action takes place in an "out of sight" way, either buried in soil or dough, or water. Clearly, this is Christ's attempt to reveal the nature of the kingdom during this time. It is not an openly physical, political, kingdom, but rather is hidden in, and works in, the hearts of men. Jesus reinforces this idea by his explanation that the seed in the parable is equivalent to the Word of God sown in the hearts of individuals (13:18-23.)

This "seed", which is entrance of the gospel into the hearts of men, or the Holy Spirit within the hearts of men, bursts into spiritual transformation of the believer in the Church Age. This was first prophesied for Israel in the future. (Acts 2:16-18; Joel 2:28-29; Isa. 28:11-12; c.p. Jer. 31:31-33; Heb. 8.) While the spiritual application of this event is certainly applicable to the present time, this does not negate the fact that these prophecies continue to have a future fulfillment for Israel. At the time the Kingdom is revealed in an outward, physical form, it will, according to Ezekiel, arise out of this inward transformation of each individual (Ez. 37:12-14.) This is clear in that Peter identifies the Pentecostal experience as that which Joel prophesied. However, he continues to quote the part of Joel's prophecy which was not fulfilled at Pentecost but which is predicted to be fulfilled in Israel's yet future revival and which will include the following:

And I will shew wonders in heaven above, and signs in the earth beneath; blood, and fire, and vapour of smoke: The

> *sun shall be turned into darkness, and the moon into blood,*
> *before the great and notable day of the Lord come: And it*
> *shall come to pass, that whosoever shall call on the name of*
> *the Lord shall be saved*
>
> −Acts 2:19-21

While there was certainly supernatural activity on the day of Pentecost, there is no record that the cosmic events described above occurred at that time. Such descriptions are not unlike numerous other Old Testament descriptions of the time of the second appearing of Christ. Nevertheless, the Holy Spirit received on the day of Pentecost was clearly the same Holy Spirit prophesied for Israel at the time of their restoration.

Not understanding the above can lead to incorrect conclusions with serious implications. An example of this mistake is evident in the following statement by Philip Mauro: "It is appropriate to point out that one of the glaring errors of "dispensational teaching" is the failure to recognize what the New Testament plainly reveals, namely that names which God temporarily gave to the shadowy and typical things of the Old Covenant, belong properly and eternally to the corresponding realities of he New Covenant. Thus, we are given the proper meaning of "Jew" (Rom. 2:28, 29); "Israel" (Rom. 9:6, Gal. 6:16), "Jerusalem" (Gal. 4:26); "Seed of Abraham" (Gal. 3:29), "Sion" (I Pet. 2:6; Heb. 12:22), Rom. 9:33) Likewise it is made known that according to the New Covenant meaning, "the tribes of Jacob" are those who are Jews inwardly, that is to say, the entire household of faith (James 1:1; Acts 26:7)."[30] We agree with Mr. Mauro that these "shadowy, and typical things of the Old Covenant, belong properly and eternally to the corresponding realities of the New Covenant." However, this does not negate the Old Testament promise of future fulfillment of the New Covenant to Israel which is attached to the second coming of Christ to rule and reign over the earth. The "mysteries" (Matt. 13) represent a *limitation* on the concept of the kingdom, as opposed to the full breadth of the future kingdom as revealed in the Old Testament. The physical promises of that Old Testament kingdom is not here, nor is it meant to be here now. The kingdom is, however, very present in the world in spiritual power to inwardly transform each individual. There is no expressed purging of nationalistic elements in this new teaching of Christ of the spiritual manifestation of the kingdom; these elements are only postponed until the kingdom comes in its fullness.[31] It has also been asserted that dispensational teachers attempt to make an arbitrary distinction between the "kingdom of Heaven" and the "kingdom of God." Admittedly, some dispensational teachers have taught that there are different ways to be saved in different dispensations. To exemplify this charge Scofield is often cited for listing four "gospels" in the notes of the "Scofield Bible." His breakdown was as follows:

a. **The gospel of the kingdom.**
This is the preaching of good news that God had promised to set up an earthly kingdom.
b. **The gospel of the grace of God.**
This is the good news of the death, burial and resurrection.
c. **The everlasting gospel.**
This is to be preached by Jews after the church is raptured, but before the beginning of the millennium, during the Tribulation period. It is the good news that those who were saved during the great tribulation will enter the millennial reign.
d. **That which Paul calls "my gospel."**
This is the gospel of grace, but has a fuller development than that preached by Christ and the apostles. Paul has given new insight into the "mystery" of the church and this is included in Paul's gospel.

The notion of multiple gospels stands in contrast, we believe, to the fact that there is only one, and will always be only one, gospel. Whether or not Scofield actually disagreed with this and was simply attempting to break down different time periods and applications of the gospel, is uncertain. Whatever the case, there is only one gospel, consisting of the good news of the Death, Burial, and Resurrection of Jesus Christ, thus effecting hope for eternal life for all mankind. This gospel is applied to believing individuals by death to sin through repentance, burial with him in baptism (Rom. 6:3), and the infilling of his Holy Spirit (Acts 2:28; Jn. 14:17-18.) There is no scriptural indication or reason to believe that this will change as long as man is in need of salvation. The completion of Christ's death, burial, and resurrection was the fulfillment of all Old Testament sacrifices and all efficacious effects which they anticipated and to which they looked forward. Communion service is held to attest to this fact, as the believer partakes of it, he declares, "…ye do shew the Lord's death till he come" (I Cor. 11:26.) Any sacrifices that succeed Christ's resurrection, should there be such, could only be viewed as a memorial that looks back to Christ's work, for "there remaineth no more sacrifice for sin." With the sin question resolved, Christ, by the indwelling of his Spirit, restores mankind back to the relationship lost in Adam's fall and described as the "New Covenant" in Heb. 8 (Is. 28:11-12; Jer. 31:31; Heb. 8; Jn. 7; 37-39; 14:17; 18; Acts 1:8; 2:1-4.) There will be no other "good news" or succeeding salvation message.

Nevertheless, it is true that though at this time the Kingdom of God has come to the earth into the spirits of men in a saving way, it has not yet come in its exterior, outward, monarchical, form.

Jesus is not yet here physically. While he is king of the believer's individual life, he does not presently physically reign as king of the world. The kingdom is now, "not meat nor drink, but righteousness, peace, and joy in the Holy Ghost" (Rom. 14:17.) It seems quite clear in scripture that entrance into the kingdom of God in any period of time since Christ's death, burial and resurrection, whether such a time be present or future, that such entrance will be by the same gospel and in the same fashion as established on the birthday of the church.

It is important to recognize that the Kingdom of God (or Heaven) is always, first and foremost, spiritual. In the Church Age it is not only "first and foremost" spiritual, but "altogether" spiritual. It is, in effect, a radically new form of human government. All previous, humanly contrived, forms of government accomplish their rule "from the outside, in." Laws exist outside of the person and are enforced compliance comes from their society. However, with the coming of individual baptism of the Holy Spirit, this changes, and now the law, for the first time in human history, comes from within, that is , is written on the tables of the heart and teaches "from within (Jer. 31:33.) (For more discussion on the Kingdom, see pages 59-62 under "Dispensation of the Church")

The parallels between the giving of the law to Moses at Sinai and the giving of the law in the hearts of men at Pentecost have been oft noted. Both have to do with "writing" the law by the finger of God—on stone at Sinai—and on the fleshy tables of the heart at Pentecost. Both were accompanied by fire and both by "languages" –"voices" at Sinai and "speaking in other tongues as the Spirit gave the utterance" at Pentecost. Both were a people becoming a nation, receiving an identity, and becoming a "royal priesthood." Jehovah declares "You will be my people, I will be your God, I will dwell amongst you and I will put my name there." At Pentecost Christ dwells in them in a way heretofore unknown. His name is officially placed upon them—by which they become his property, his children—through water baptism and subsequent Spirit infilling.

It is interesting that Jeremiah specifies that the law would be written in their "hearts." The heart, in such usage, means the mind and the seat of emotions, that is, the will. General law of right and wrong is already written in the mind via the conscience. But this is not the same thing. The law written in the human heart clearly points to a *desire* and *determination* to do what is right. One does it of his own volition. Rather than onerous duty, it becomes acts of love for one's deliverer, and thus is no longer bondage, but rather elevates obedience from duty of law to liberation of love. The Spirit on the inside **enables** the individual to do what is known to be right. Salvation conquers sins perverse power not only in the universe but also within the individual.

This is nothing short of radical. In such a setting of daily life on earth, the need of outward governmental structure is dramatically reduced. Taxes are lowered as the need of law enforcement is reduced. Locksmiths, gun dealers, alarm companies, fences builders, health care providers, protection agencies, military expenditures, and such like—all multimillion-dollar industries, are reduced to negligible size—all because the law is written in the heart of each individual. The point is that the effect of individual salvation on a worldwide scale is the creation of the kingdom of heaven on earth. The point of origin of all this is the spiritual kingdom coming into the hearts of people who are spiritually "born again" (John 3:3, 5.)

In the early church, as noted above, the consummation of the message of the Death, Burial, and Resurrection of Jesus resulted in persons individually experiencing the Spirit of Christ within them (Jn. 4:24; 14:17-18; Acts 2:1-4; Rom. 8:9.) This reception of the Spirit was "the law being written on their hearts" in fulfillment of Jeremiah's prophecy and was the norm for each individual believer. Again, repentance (death to sin) equated to the death of Jesus being applied to the individual believer. Water baptism equaled the believer joining with Christ in his burial and "being buried with Him" (Rom. 6:3-8.) Receiving the Holy Spirit paralleled, in the recipient's life, the resurrection of Jesus. This "new birth", or resurrection, was, and is, Christ literally infilling and infusing each individual with his victorious life (Jn. 7:37-39.) The believer experienced Christ's resurrection, not simply as a symbol, but an actual entering into Christ's resurrection. Thus, for the believer in the Church Age, the message is "believe and obey the gospel, for Jesus is coming to catch away his church!" (I Thess. 1:7-8; I Cor. 15:22-23, 51-52; I Thes. 4:15-17.)

The time immediately following the Church Age is described by Jesus in Matthew 24:1-32. He identifies this period as the time of "great tribulation" (v. 21.) Israel as a nation, after having been deceived, and accepting the Antichrist as the Messiah (Jn. 5:43), will recognize that the Antichrist is not the Messiah, and will consequently turn to Christ. The nation will then finally fulfill its calling to act as the conduit of God's message of salvation to the remaining world (Gen. 12:3; Ps. 67; Mt. 24:14; Rom. 11:15.) According to the many prophecies of the Old Testament, they will believe and obey the gospel and will proclaim the coming of the Messiah to bring justice, peace, and righteous judgment to the nations wherein he will reign as King of Kings on the earth!" (Mt. 25:31-34; Rev. 19.) Though this is a different announcement of a different prophetic event, the application of the gospel message to the individual remains the same.

Revelation 14:6 contains a reference to the "everlasting gospel." Some, like Scofield, have taken this to mean another "gospel" than the gospel as we know it. However, the descriptor itself ("everlasting gospel") appears to reinforce the fact that there is only one gospel and that it is everlasting. To assume that the Death, Burial, and Resurrection, or its application to the individual as described above, is going to be replaced or superseded by something else, seems unwarranted. To assume that the application of that gospel to the individual is going to vary in any age from the pattern given in Joel 2:25-29; Ez. 37:12-14; Acts 2:1-4, 38, etc., seems to equally lack foundation. In contrast, Peter makes clear on the Day of Pentecost that what they received, was, in fact, the spiritual promise that was prophesied by Joel to be for the nation of Israel (Acts 2:16-21.)

The apostle Paul calls the gospel "my gospel." In his scheme, Scofield identified this as a sort of "fourth gospel." He acknowledges it as being "the gospel of grace, but has a fuller development than that preached by Christ and the apostles." In regards to this, we would say that, to identify the phrase "my gospel" as being "another gospel", is, at best, a poor differentiation, and at worst, simply wrong. Again, there is only one gospel. While Paul was, indeed, declaring additional insight into the nature and character of the church, this does not equate to "another gospel."

Dispensations and "Hyper-Literalism"

It has already been discussed that dispensational teaching is based upon the belief that scripture should always be interpreted as first meaning what it says. While it may always mean more, it will never mean less. Thus the many Old Testament promises of a future and permanent establishment of Israel in their land are to be taken first as they are written and to mean what they plainly say. Though Bible writers utilized a wide variety of linguistic devices with which to communicate (metaphor, simile, symbol, type, poem, hymn, figure, etc) one cannot therefore arbitrarily decide that a plain statement should be interpreted allegorically instead of literally.

On the other hand, there are those who go beyond a healthy definition of "literal" and some of the charges leveled in this regard have validity.

An example of this "hyper-literalism" is the rigid claim that some scriptures apply exclusively to given time periods and therefore lack any applicability to other time periods. The assertion is that scriptures have been given "dispensationally", and different passages of the Bible are exclusively directed to different dispensations. In such teaching, Israel and the church are two distinct bodies and very little of the Old Testament has to do with the church. The following statement by W.L. Pettingill is an example: "I have long been convinced, and have taught, that the Great Commission of Mt. 28:19 is primarily applicable to the Kingdom rather than to the church… The Matthew commission will come into force for the Jewish remnant after the church is caught away."[32]

Statements such as that above by Pettingill, are not only misleading, but seem to arise out of the idea previously discussed of "multiple gospels." If the church is preaching one gospel and the future Jewish remnant another, then such dissection has some appearance of being plausible. However, the simple truth is that there is only one gospel, whether for Church in the present or national Israel in the future. Further, the mandate for propagating that gospel is the same regardless of time frame. Thus, Matthew 28:19 certainly belongs to the present as much as it does to the future. This inclusive method of interpretation is not an "exception" to normal interpretation, but is the norm. What is here true of the applicability of Matthew 28:19 is equally true of scores of other scriptures, such as Joel 2:28-29; Is. 28:11-12; Jer. 31:33, the Beatitudes (Mt. 5, 6, 7), etc. These scriptures belong to all who obey the gospel, whether past, present, or future.

Dispensations and Artificial Divisions In The Bible

Another oft repeated allegation is that dispensational teaching creates divisions that are humanly devised and that dispensations are, in effect, constructs which may be helpful but are nevertheless artificial. However, only a cursory inspection is required to see that these epochal shifts are obvious in scripture and certainly not "artificial." In fact, these distinctions, differences, contrasts and progressive movements can hardly be ignored if one is going to seriously attempt to unpack the biblical message. For example, it is unrealistic not to note the self-evident differences between the hundreds of details in the Mosaic sacrificial system as opposed to the simpler and earlier Noahic period. While there are variations in how interpreters define these distinctions, there is no interpreter of the Bible who does not recognize the need for, and reality of, basic distinctions in the Scriptures. The non-dispensationalist theologian, for all his opposition to dispensationalism, also makes certain rather important distinctions. For example, Berkof, after rejecting the usual dispensational scheme of Bible distinctions, enumerates his own scheme of dispensations or administrations, reducing the number to two—the Old Testament dispensation and the New Testament dispensation. However, within the Old Testament dispensation he lists four subdivisions that, although he terms "stages in the revelation of the covenant of grace," are distinguishable enough to be listed.[33] Thus the covenant theologian (i.e., "non-dispensationalist") finds Biblical distinctions a necessary part of his theology just as does those who recognize and categorize the dispensations.[34]

A primary objective in dispensational study is to unveil the fact of a universal, progressive revelation of God to man and the divine intent to bring universal redemption. The important role which even imperfect dispensational teaching has played in bringing people to recognition of this progressive revelation is recognized by scholars, some of whom would not be thought of as embracing a dispensationalist position. For example, Bernard Ramm, even though not a dispensationalist, admitted that a clearer realization of progressive revelation has been largely due to the "beneficial influence of dispensationalism."[35] Commenting on those scholars who espoused and taught dispensational teaching, George Ladd adds: "It is doubtful if there has been any other circle of men who have done more by their influence in preaching, teaching, and writing to promote a love for Bible study, a hunger for the deeper Christian life, a passion for evangelism and zeal for missions in the history of American Christianity."[36] The fact is that dispensations are so obvious that they have been recognized (as we shall see below) from the earliest days of the church until now.

Dispensational Teaching—Origins

A widespread—but seriously incorrect—assumption is that dispensational teaching is of recent origin (early 1800's) and had for its founder a Plymouth Brethren minister named John Darby.

One of the original and primary protests against dispensational teaching was that it was "modernistic." The accusation was that, being of recent origin, it lacked historical validity.

While the source of such assumptions may be obscure, it is probable that a book by Philip Mauro (1859-1952) has been a primary source. The book, entitled "The Gospel of the Kingdom" (1929) had considerable influence, and was apparently quoted by others who evidently did not verify Mauro's statements before using them. Ehlert, speaking of Mauro, a lawyer and rabid opponent of dispensational teaching, states; "It is obvious throughout the book that Mr. Mauro knew absolutely nothing of any dispensationalism before Darby, for he says, 'The entire system of dispensational teaching is modernistic in the strictest sense; for it first came into existence within the memory of persons now living and was altogether unknown even in their younger days.'[37] George E. Ladd, obviously trusting this or other mistaken sources, declares: "For all practical purposes we may consider that…dispensationalism…had its source with Darby and Kelly."[38] However, as shown below, this is an incorrect conclusion.

Many citations are available which show the long history of teaching which validates the recognition of dispensations or the rudiments thereof from earliest days of the church. Below are a few of these citations.

- It has been noted that **Clement of Alexandria**, as early as (150-220) pluralizes the "the patriarchal dispensation, "distinguishing clearly three patriarchal dispensations, as given in Adam, Noah, and Abraham; then comes the Mosaic."

- **Pelagius and Cooelestius** taken to task by Augustine for "dividing the times: as to say that "men first lived righteously by nature, then under the law, thirdly under grace...For then, say they, the Creator was known by the guidance of reason; and the rule of living rightly was carried written in the hearts of men, not by the law of the letter, but of nature. When men's manners became corrupt; and then, they say, when nature now tarnished began to be in sufficient the law was added...but after the habit of sinning had too much prevailed among men, and the law was unequal to the task of curing it, Christ came;..."

- **Augustine** himself, though disputing with those listed above concerning dispensations, nevertheless declares; "The divine institution of sacrifice was suitable in the former dispensation, but is not suitable now." He goes on to declare: "For the change suitable to the present age has been enjoined by God, who knows infinitely better than man what is fitting for every age...ordering all events in His providence until the beauty of the completed course of time, the component parts of which are the dispensations adapted to each successive age, shall be finished, like the grand melody of some ineffably wise master of song, and those pass into the eternal contemplation of God who here, though it is a time of faith, not of sight, are acceptably worshipping him."[39]

- **William Cave** (1637-1713) included an introductory discourse on the three major dispensations:
  I. Patriarchal, from the beginning of the world till the delivery of the law upon Mt. Sinai
  II. Mosaical, from the delivery of the law till the final period of the Jewish state.
  III. Evangelical, to last to the end of the world[40]

- **Pierre Poiret** (1649-1719) a French mystic and philosopher who wrote more than 40 works of great import to French theological thought, attempted to comprehend, like many others, the whole story of redemption. His great work *L'OEconomie Divine,* first published in Amsterdam in 1687 was rendered into English and published in London in 1713. It clearly contains a dispensational scheme. He uses the phrase "period of dispensation" and his seventh dispensation is a literal thousand-year millennium with Christ returned and reigning in bodily form upon the earth with His saints and with Israel regathered and converted. He also sees the rise of the Antichrist, the two resurrections and many of the general run of end-time events. He declared: "Tho' I do not pretend precisely to determine the Number nor Duration of these Periods, it is obvious however unto all, that the World hath really passed thro' Periods of this Nature."[41] Poiret's outline of dispensations, while preceding Darby by more than one hundred years, contained virtually the same outline and clearly indicates, along with others, that the dispensations of the Bible were long recognized throughout history.

- **John Edwards** (1639-1716) wrote the first extensive treatise on the subject of dispensations. He was an eminent English Calvinist. In his preface, he states: "I have undertaken a Great Work, viz, to display all the Transactions of Divine Providence relating to the Methods of Religion, from the Creation to the end of the World, from the first Chapter of Genesis to the last of the Revelation. For Id not met with any author that had undertaken to comprise them all, and to give us a true account of them according to their true series: nor had I ever lit upon a writer who had designedly traced the particular causes and grounds of them or settled them in their right and true foundations. Wherefore I betook myself to this work, resolving to attempt something, though it were only to invite others of greater skill to go on with it." From this quote it appears that there was a literature on the subject at that early date, which could probably still be examined at the Cambridge libraries. Edwards' scheme was:

  I.   Innocency and Felicity, or Adam created upright
  II. Sin and Misery, Adam fallen

III. Reconcilation, or Adam recovered, from Adam's re-demption to the end of the World, "The discovery of the blessed seed of Adam":
   a. Patriarchal economy:
      1. Adamical, antediluvian
      2. Noahical
      3. Abrahamic
   b. Mosaical
   c. Gentile (concurrent with "a" and "b")
   d. Christian or Evangelical:
      1. Infancy, primitive period, past
      2. Childhood, present
      3. Manhood, future
      4. Old age, from the loosing of Satan to the con-flagration[42]

- **John Shute Barrington**, (1678-1734) was a friend and disciple of Locke. Barrington had an essay on "The Dispensations of God to Mankind as Revealed in Scripture" which included;

   I.   The State of Innocence
   II.   Patriarchal
   III. Noahic
   IV.   Abrahamic
   V.   Noahic[43]

- **Isaac Watts** (1674-1748.) The great hymn writer was also a theo-logian. He wrote an essay of some 40 pages entitled "The Harmony of all the Religions which God ever prescribed to men and all his dispensations towards them." His definition of "dispensations" was, "The public dispensations of God towards men, are those wise and holy constitutions of his will and government, revealed or some way manifested to them, in the several successive periods or ages of the world, wherein are contained the duties which he expects from men, and the blessings which he promises, or encourages them to expect from him, here and hereafter; together with the sins which he forbids, and the punishments which he threatens to inflict on such sinners: Or the dispensations of God may be described more briefly, as the appointed moral rules of God's dealing with mankind, considered as reasonable creatures, and as accountable to him for their behaviour, both in this world and in that which is to come. Each of these dispensations of God, may be represented as different religions, or, at least, as different forms of religion, appointed for men in the several successive ages of the world."[44] His outline was:

I. The Dispensation of Innocency, or, the Religion of Adam at first

II. The Adamical Dispensation of the Covenant of Grace, or the Religion of Adam after his Fall

III. The Noahical Dispensation; or, the Religion of Noah

IV. The Abrahamical Dispensation; or, the Religion of Abraham

V. The Mosaical Dispensation, or, the Jewish Religion

VI. The Christian Dispensation

It becomes evident at once, of course, that this is exactly the outline of the first six dispensations that has been so widely publicized by C.I. Scofield in the notes in the "Scofield" Bible.

- **Jonathan Edwards** (1703-1758.) Edwards, while not writing a scheme of dispensations to the extent of others, does recognize epochal movements, and does use the word "dispensations" in stating: "The various dispensations of works...are but the several parts of one scheme...all the various dispensations that belong to it are united; and the several wheels are one machine, to answer one end, and produce on effect."[45]

- **John Fletcher** (1729-1785.) An intimate friend of the Wesley's, Fletcher was known for his piety and also developed an order of dispensations. He described his reasoning: "If a judicious mariner, who has sailed around the world, sees with pleasure a map, which exhibits, in one point of view, the shape and proportion of the wide seas…a judicious Protestant may profitably look upon a doctrinal map (if I may be allowed the expression)…more especially if this map exhibits, with some degree of accuracy, the boundaries of truth…Without any apology, therefore, I shall lay before the reader a plain account of the primitive catholic Gospel, and its various dispensations." He then identifies six dispensations. Following the second coming of Christ there will be "another Gospel dispensation" which we have now in prophecy, "as the Jews had the Gospel of Christ's first advent, during which the Church reigns with Christ for a thousand years. Fletcher equates this event to the "restitution of all things."[46]

The citations of those who saw and understood the dispensations is much, much, longer than what is listed here. Also, the list of those who understood and taught a future Millennium is longer still and extends far back into antiquity. While the number of dispensations sometimes varied according to how they were grouped, they were nevertheless generally recognized and acknowledged by scholars and theologians from virtually every background, including Church of England, Puritan heritage, Quaker heritage, Presbyterian, Episcopalian, Unitarian, Irvingite, Scottish, Dutch, etc. and include such as both Robert Jamieson and Canon Fausset (of Jamieson, Fausset, and Brown Commentary, fame), Samuel Hanson Cox, one of the founders of the Union Theological Seminary, New York, and many others.

Interestingly, the sixth dispensation in John Darby's scheme, rather than being called the "Church Age", was called "The Age of the Spirit."[47]

Dispensations And Daniel's 70th Week

It was told the prophet Daniel that "seventy weeks are determined upon thy people and upon thy holy city..." (Dan. 9:24.) History reveals that the period of time from the beginning of the seventy weeks until their consummation with Christ's coming revelation on the Mt. of Olives, is the "Times of the Gentiles", or, the time in which Gentile powers rule over Israel. The purpose of the seventy weeks was:

a. To finish the transgression
b. To make an end of sins
c. To make reconciliation for iniquity
d. To bring in everlasting righteousness
e. To seal up the vision and prophecy
f. To anoint the most Holy

It may not be possible to know if the above six points were given to Daniel in the order in which they would be fulfilled. However, it is not unreasonable to assume that they were. It is evident that the first three (a, b, and c) were accomplished at Calvary. In a way, it would also be correct to say that all six points were accomplished at Calvary, even though the complete outworking of this accomplishment is not yet fulfilled. There is clearly a fulfilling of "d", "e", and "f", which has not yet occurred, but will occur at the conclusion of Daniel's 70th week with the revelation of Christ in which every eye will see him (Mt. 24:29-30; Rev. 19.) With his coming, and victorious triumph (Rev. 19) Christ will "bring in everlasting righteousness" as well as being acknowledged and anointed as the "most Holy" by the nations of the world (Ps. 67; 2:8-12; 22:26-31; Is. 49:6-13; 60:3.)

The seventy weeks was explained to Daniel as follows:

a. This time period of weeks would begin with the going forth of the commandment to restore and to build Jerusalem. This, according to Nehemiah 2, places the date at 445 B.C.)
b. Up until the time of the Messiah shall be 69 weeks (The 70

Weeks are obviously weeks of years. It was thus 483 years from the time 445 B.C. to Jesus the Messiah being cut off (v. 26.)

c. After the end of the 69 weeks, the city shall be destroyed and the sanctuary (v. 26)

d. The end of the 69 weeks "shall be with a flood, and unto the end of the war desolations are determined" (v. 26. Desolations are determined on Israel "unto the end of the war", i.e., on Israel)

e. The antichrist shall confirm a covenant of peace with Israel at the beginning of the 70th week. In the midst of the week he breaks the covenant (v. 27.) Then ensues the "overspreading of abomina-tions" (Mt. 24:15, 21) in which "he shall make it desolate, even until the consummation…"(v. 27.) This "desolation" began at the conclusion of the 69th week, (which occurred when the Jews rejected Jesus) and is the period of time between the end of the 69th week and the conclusion of the 70th week. The 70th week is identified by Jesus as a time of "great tribulation", and is also called the time of "Jacob's trouble"(not a time of the "churches' trouble.") It is a desolation on Israel, (Rom. 11:11, 19, 24) Christ, at the end of this desolation, shall "…inherit the desolate heri-tages" (Is. 49:8.) The events of Daniel's 70th week as described by Christ are recorded in Matthew 24:1-31 and also Revelation, chapters 6-19 as well as numerous Old Testament scriptures.

Christ's triumphal return (Rev. 19) brings a firm conclusion to Daniel's seventy weeks (i.e., concluding the period of time in which Gentles have dominion of Israel, or the "Times of the Gentiles.") In terms of the nation of Israel, this is the primary reason for His coming, that is, to conclude the period of Gentile rule over them, and reestablish them as the "head and not the tail" among the nations. Restored Israel will reign with him over the Gentiles. However, this will not be a "bad" thing for the Gentiles, but rather they will be blessed by the original order designed by God (Rom. 11:12, 15.) In fact, seeing the benefits, the Gentile nations will ac-tually provide assistance to Israel in their reestablishment. (Is. 14:2; 49:22; 43:6; 60:4-9; 66:19-20; 2:1-4.) The Messiah will reign as King of Kings, and, as such, will restore Israel to their originally intended position.

Dispensations And The Case For A Restored Israel

When reading the literature of those who deny a restoration of national Israel, one can, over a period of time, lose sight of the number of scriptures that predict the revival of, and return of Jews. The evidence for their restoration is overwhelming. Below are a few of these scriptures.

I. Promises of a Restoration of National Israel:

For the Lord will have mercy on Jacob, and will yet choose Israel, and set them in their own land: and the strangers shall be joined with them, and they shall cleave to the house of Jacob. And the people shall take them and bring them to their place; and the house of Israel shall possess them in the land of the Lord for servants and handmaids: and they shall take them captives, whose captives they were: and they shall rule over their oppressors.

–Isaiah 14:1-2

And it shall come to pass in that day, that the Lord shall beat off from the channel of the river unto the stream of Egypt, and ye shall be gathered one by one, O ye children of Israel.

–Isaiah 27:12

Therefore, behold, the days come, saith the Lord, that it shall no more be said, The Lord liveth that brought up the children of Israel out of the land of Egypt. But the Lord liveth that brought up the children of Israel from the land of the north, and from all the lands whither he had driven them: and I will bring them again into their land that I gave unto their fathers.

–Jeremiah 16:14-15

For, lo, the days come, saith the Lord, that I will bring again

the captivity of my people Israel and Judah, saith the Lord:
and I will cause them to return to the land that I gave to their
fathers, and they shall possess it.

–Jeremiah 30:3

Hear the word of the Lord, O ye nations, and declare it in the
isles afar off, and say, He that scattered Israel will gather him,
and keep him, as a shepherd doth his flock.

–Jeremiah 30:10

But Judah shall dwell forever, and Jerusalem from generation
to generation.

–Joel 3:20

And I will bring again the captivity of my people of Israel,
and they shall build the waste cities, and inhabit them; and
they shall plant vineyards, and drink the wine thereof; they
shall also make gardens, and eat the fruit of them.

–Amos 9:14

In that day, saith the Lord, will I assemble her that halteth,
and I will gather her that is driven out, and her that I have
afflicted; And I will make her that halted a remnant, and her
that was cast far off a strong nation: and the Lord shall reign
over them in mount Zion from henceforth, even for ever.

–Micah 4:6, 7

Many other scriptures include: Isaiah 43:5-6; 49:8-12; Jer. 23:3-8; 30:3, l0, 11; 31:8; Zeph. 3:14-20; Ezek. 11:17-21; 20:33-44; 34:11-13; 14-16; ch. 37; 36:16-37; 39:25-39; Zech. 8:7-8; 10:6, 8.

Perhaps special note should be made of the graphic and unmistakable description of Israel's restoration as recorded by the prophet Ezekiel (chapter 37.) Israel is here depicted as a graveyard of a defeated people, the bones of which have long lain latent and which, when found in chapter 37, are now very desiccated, very dry, and very many. The unique description of their restoration to life is some of the world's finest literature. The entirety of those in the graveyard are raised (by prophetic preaching) to robust life in the most dramatic and startling fashion. The prophet is plainly told:

> *Son of man, these bones are the whole house of Israel; behold, they say, Our bones are dried, and our hope is lost; we are cut off for our parts. Therefore prophesy and say unto them, Thus saith the Lord God, Behold, O my people, I will open your graves, and cause you to come up out of your graves, and bring you into the land of Israel. And shall put my Spirit in you, and ye shall live, and I shall place you in your own land: then shall ye know that I the Lord have spoken it, and performed it, saith the Lord. And say unto them, Thus saith the Lord God; Behold, I will take the children of Israel from among the heathen, whither they be gone, and will gather them on every side, and bring them into their own land. And I will make them one nation in the land upon the mountains of Israel; and one king shall be king to them all: and they shall be no more two nations, neither shall they be divided into kingdoms anymore at all. Moreover I will make a covenant of peace with them; it shall be an everlasting covenant with them; and I will place them, and multiply them, and will set my sanctuary in the midst of them forevermore. My tabernacle also shall be with them; yea, I will be their God, and they shall be my people. And the heathen shall know that I the Lord do sanctify Israel, when my sanctuary shall be in the midst of them forevermore.*
> -Ezekiel 37:11-12, 14, 19, 21, 22, 26-27

This graphic, detailed, and explicit prophecy of Israel's restoration is difficult to ignore.

II. ISRAEL WILL LEAD THE WORLD AND JERUSALEM WILL BE THE WORLD-CAPITAL IN THE MILLENIUM

with Christ, the Son of David, as King (Jer. 3:17; Ez. 48:35; Is. 60:14; 62:12; Mal. 3:1; Ps. 48:2; Ps. 46:4; Ez. 47:1; Joel 3:18; Zech. 14:8; Is. 60:1-3.) Christ will rule over all. (Ps. 72:8-11; Zech. 14:9; Is. 9:7; 11:1-9; Jer. 23:5-6; 33:24-17; Ez. 37:21-27; Micah 4:7; Ex. 9:6)

Israel was God's 'corporate' son, and is identified as God's son numerous times in the Old Testament. The parallels between Israel and Christ, the incarnate son, are remarkable. Upon crossing the Red Sea, Israel is confronted with the jolting implications of being God's chosen medium for manifesting himself to the world. On the mount at SinaI they receive an identity (Ex. 19:4, 5), and a mission, or calling (Ex. 19:6) and are driven into the wilderness. All of this comes in deep and grave fashion. Likewise, at his baptism, and then on the mount of temptation, the incarnate Son receives an identity and mission (Mk. 1:10-11) and is immediately driven into the wilderness (v. 12.) Like Israel, this comes in deep and sobering fashion.

Both experience a spiritual formation in the wilderness, which, in scripture, is a place of chaos, undomesticated and wild, the haunt of the demonic. Along with "the deep", and high mountains, the wilderness represents the place of the "wild-er", the uninhabited (by man), the untamed, the feral. Both the corporate son and the incarnate son must conquer the wilderness before accomplishing their mission.

Israel, the corporate son, is a real people. They go into a physical as well as a spiritual wilderness. Jesus, the incarnate son, likewise, goes physically as well as spiritually into the wilderness. Both are historical realities. Israel dies, disappears as a nation, but is promised a resurrection (Ex. 37.) Christ dies, and is buried, but is promised a resurrection and does resurrect physically and is taken up from them physically (Acts 1:9.) The two angels then emphatically state "this same Jesus, which is taken up from you into heaven, shall so come in like manner as ye have seen him go into heaven." Thus, in fulfillment of numerous prophecies, Christ is born physically, lives physically upon the earth, dies physically, is physically buried, and resurrects physically. The angels then declare that he shall return physically, that is, "in like manner" as he is taken up. To deny this actual, physical, return is to fly directly in the face of plain scriptural statements. Thus the many prophecies of Christ were all *literally* fulfilled, and were not simply *symbolic* or *allegorical*, but were real events, which happened in real-time. The fact that this fulfillment of prophecies concerning the human Son came from the same Old Testament from which also come the prophecies of the restoration of Israel (the corporate son) provides us with the knowledge of how such prophecies are also to be fulfilled.

Jesus is, then, as the Jewish Messiah, both the incarnation of Israel's final success as well as the leader of that success. As such he personally fulfills all that Israel was intended to be. However, he absolutely refuses to accept this position alone, but repeatedly insists on bringing his people with him. Psalm 22, the crucifixion Psalm, records this determination several times (as do numerous other scriptures):

> *I will declare thy name unto my brethren: in the midst of the congregation will I praise thee." (v. 22)*

In the next verse, he then encourages Israel that he will not fail to bring them with him.

> *Ye that fear the Lord, praise him; all ye the seed of Jacob, glorify him; and fear him, all ye the seed of Israel. (v. 23)*

Christ's radical determination to accomplish not only an individual victory, but also a corporate victory, is seen again in v. 25:

> *My praise shall be of thee in the great congregation: I will pay my vows before them that fear him.*

Again, in v. 27, he reveals that not only Israel, but;

> *All the ends of the world shall remember and turn unto the Lord and all the kindreds of the nations shall worship before thee.*

In the final two verses of the Psalm, he repeats his insistence that he will not accept a personal victory separate from a corporate victory when he declares: *"A seed shall serve him; it shall be accounted to the Lord for a generation. They shall come, and shall declare his righteousness unto a people that shall be born, that he hath done this."*

When Christ brings his people with him, as seen above, it includes not only Israel, but also the nations of the world. However, the saving of the whole world does nothing to negate the exclusive promises given to Israel regarding their nationhood and their land. In fact, as Paul makes clear (Rom. 11:15), Christ will accomplish this blessing to the whole world by means of Israel itself; *"For if the casting away of them be the reconciling of the world,* (i.e, during the church age), *what shall the receiving of them be but life from the dead?"* (i.e., the time of the spiritual renewal of Israel as recorded in Ezekiel 37.) Joel declares: *"But Judah shall dwell forever, and Jerusalem from generation to generation."* (3:20.) Israel, having existed as a nation in history, certainly preserved the hope and expectation that it would again do so. Ezekiel's emphasis on this can hardly be overlooked and merits being here quoted:

> *Then he said unto me, Son of man, these bones are the whole house of Israel: behold, they say, Our bones are dried, and our hope is lost: we are cut off for our parts.*
>
> *Therefore prophesy and say unto them, Thus saith the Lord God; Behold, O my people, I will open your graves, and cause you to come up out of your graves, and bring you in to the land of Israel. And ye shall know that I am the Lord, when I have opened your graves, O my people, and brought you up out of your graves. And shall put my spirit in you, and ye shall live, and I shall place you in your own land: then shall ye know that I the Lord have spoken it, and performed it, saith the Lord.*
>
> *And say unto them, Thus saith the Lord God; Behold, I will*

take the children of Israel from among the heathen, whither they be gone, and will gather them on every side, and bring them into their own land: And I will make them one nation in the land upon the mountains of Israel; and one king shall be king to them all; and they shall be no more two nations, neither shall they be divided into two kingdoms any more at all. Neither shall they defile themselves any more with their idols, nor with their detestable things, nor with any of their transgressions: but I will save them out of all their dwelling-places, wherein they have sinned and will cleanse them: so shall they be my people, and I will be their God. And David my servant shall be king over them; and they all shall have one shepherd: they shall also walk in my judgments, and observe my statues, and do them. And they shall dwell in the land that I have given unto Jacob my servant, wherein your fathers have dwelt; and they shall dwell therein, even they, and their children, and their children's children forever; and my servant David shall be their prince for ever. Moreover I will make a covenant of peace with them; it shall be an everlasting covenant with them: and I will place them, and multiply them, and will set my sanctuary in the midst of them for evermore. My tabernacle also shall be with them: yea, I will be their God, and they shall be my people. And the heathen shall know that I the Lord do sanctify Israel, when my sanctuary shall be in the midst of them for evermore.

–Ezek. 37:1-14, 21-28

Passages which reveal further details regarding Israel's future include both their spiritual (Ez. 20:41; 28:25; 36:22-23; 37:28; 39:21, 23; Is. 45:14; 49:26) as well as natural renewal, and includes a renewal of nature itself (Is. 32:15, 20; Ez. 34:26-27, 29; Amos 9:13-14; Ez. 34:29 (known for her crops), Is. 35:9, including the threat of wild beasts being removed (Ez. 34:25 Is. 11:6-9; 65:25; Hos. 2:18.))

In the New Testament, Jesus declares to the disciples:

Ye which have followed me, in the regeneration when the
Son of man shall sit in the throne of his glory, ye also shall sit
upon twelve thrones, judging the twelve tribes of Israel.

–Mt. 19:28

In speaking to the city of Jerusalem he laments:

Behold, your house is left unto you desolate. For I say unto
you, Ye shall not see me henceforth, till yet shall say, Blessed is
he that cometh in the name of the Lord.

–Mt. 23:38-39

He further provides the disciples the promise that:

...I appoint unto you a kingdom, as my Father hath appointed
unto me; That ye may eat and drink at my table in my king-
dom, and sit on thrones judging the twelve tribes of Israel.

–Luke 22:29-30

Numerous other scriptures make the fact clear of a coming messianic kingdom. (Lk. 13:29; 14:15; Acts 1:6-7; 3:19-21; II Tim. 2:12; I Cor. 6:1-3; Rev. 3:21)

The apostle Paul, in the New Testament, reiterates that Israel's present unbelief does not remove God's determination and faithfulness to fulfill his covenant promises to Israel (Rom. 3:1-4.) In chapter 9, verses 1-3, he includes the covenants and promises as being among the possessions of the people of Israel. "Covenants" and "promises" surely includes the various covenants made with Abraham, the nation, David and the promise of the new covenant. It would also appear that "the promises" the apostle references would clearly include the promises given to Abraham, Isaac, Jacob, Moses, Israel, and David, all of which include the land of Israel.

Following the completion of the millennium, a new heaven and new earth is predicted which shall be a final state of perfection. (Is. 60:19-20; 65:17; 66:22; Rev. 21:23; 22:5; Is. 54:11-12.)

Dispensations And Preterism

Much erroneous teaching of prophetic scripture is derived from two basic false assumptions regarding the nation of Israel. One is the idea that, with the coming of the church, God's dealings with Israel is finished. This error comes packaged in a variety of ways, but always with the same basic premise, that is, the Church is now Israel and the many scriptures which make promises to Israel now apply to the church. Proponents of this teaching often consider natural Jews as enemies who are attempting to prevent the church from fulfilling its rightful position in replacing the natural Jews as God's chosen people. One form of this doctrine is often referred to as "Preterism."

"Preterism" comes from the word "preterite", which means "something existing in the past." Eschatologically, preterism is the doctrine that the book of Revelation, and by association, all other apocalyptic literature, has already been fulfilled sometime in the past (i.e., before our time.) While there are variations of the doctrine, some of its main tenets, as well as a brief response to each, are listed below.

Preterism Claim #1: The predictions of Jesus regarding the end-time as recorded in Matthew 24 and Luke 21 were completely fulfilled in 70 A.D. with the destruction of Jerusalem by the Romans.

Response: Matthew 24 and Luke 21 contain teaching of Jesus to his disciples which came on the heels of his announcement of judgment upon Jerusalem (Mt. 23:37-39.) He informs his disciples that the consequence of his rejection in Jerusalem will be a judgment on the city in which not one stone will be left upon another (24:1, 2.) The disciples then ask three questions which are:

a. When shall these things be,
b. what shall be the sign of thy coming, and
c. of the end of the world, or age (24:2.)

The remainder of chapter twenty-four as well as chapter twenty-five is the response of Jesus to these questions.

The preterist position is that the descriptions of judgment in these chapters, as well as in the book of Revelation, were all completely and finally fulfilled with the destruction of Jerusalem by the Romans in 70 A.D. In the preterist explanation, no room is given for discussion of the nature of virtually all prophetic scripture. Further, in attempts to make verses "match up", those verses which obviously reference events which do not fit the 70 A.D. judgment on Jerusalem are often forced into strained interpretations.

In answering the disciples questions Jesus described both the events surrounding the soon destruction of Jerusalem as well as the events which will surround his coming and the end of the age. Regarding the destruction of Jerusalem, history records how those happenings paralleled the predictions of Jesus. However, he clearly predicted other things which did not refer to the destruction of Jerusalem in 70 A.D., but were descriptions of events yet future.

An example of this is that the disciples asked for a specific "sign" that would be a signal of his coming. The sign which Jesus gives is found in verses 14 and 15 of Matthew 24 and read as follows: "When ye therefore shall see the abomination of desolation, spoken of by Daniel the prophet, stand in the holy place, (whoso readeth let him understand): Then let them which be in Judea flee into the mountains…"

This scripture is a reference to the time, in the middle of the 70th week of Daniel, when the antichrist, whom the Jews will have accepted as the Messiah (Jn. 5:43) will place an image of himself to be worshipped as God, in the temple at Jerusalem. This will be violently against all the Jews know about putting images in the temple. At that point of the Great Tribulation, the Jews will recognize that they have been deceived. In turn, the wrath and hatred of the antichrist against the Jews will become open, at which time he will radically and quickly turn on them. Jesus here reveals to us that this will happen so quickly that, to survive, the inhabitants of Judea will not have time to do anything but immediately flee. At the destruction of the temple in Jerusalem in 70 A.D., the antichrist did not set up an image of himself in the temple as spoken of by the prophet Daniel.

Preterism Claim #2: The destruction of Jerusalem in 70 A.D. was the fulfillment of Daniels 70th week, thus, there is no gap between the 69th and 70th week of Daniel 9.

Response: Jesus declared that the great tribulation time would be "such as was not since the beginning of the world to this time, no, nor ever shall be" (v. 21.) The Preterist position is hard pressed to validate any claims that 70 A.D. matched this description. In terms of world calamities, history records many tragic events which would far supersede the 70 A.D. destruction of Jerusalem. Contrariwise, history records that even other Jewish defeats were, in fact, worse For example, the revolt of Bar Kokba a few decades later was at least of the same tragic degree as the 70 A.D. sack of Jerusalem. A case can also be made that the defeat of the Jews at the Battle of Carchemish in 586 B.C., was much more devastating than the fall of Jerusalem in 70 A.D. Again, Jesus doesn't limit the severity of this tribulation to only a Jewish holocaust, but declares it to be the greatest tribulation since the beginning of the world. Estimates are that a maximum of perhaps 600,000 Jews were killed in the conflict of 66-70 A.D. The assertion that this was the world's greatest tribulation could be made only by one who lacks knowledge of world history. Further, when asked about the slaughter of 4 million Jews in the NazI holocaust, some preterists assert that the holocaust has been exaggerated.

Preterism Claim #3: Satan is bound during this, the church age.

Response: The idea that Satan is presently bound in the church age is a position which simply does not match the clear revelation of scripture. Scriptures such as those following make very clear that Satan is certainly active during this, the Church age (I Cor. 5:3; 7:5;

4:3-4; II Cor. 11:14; 12:7; I Thes. 2:18, etc.) With world conditions as they presently are, with the vicious devastation of sin everywhere visible, it is difficult to imagine this being the case. The assertion that Satan is presently bound, or has been bound during the church age, is, in itself, an incredible assertion.

Preterism Claim #4: The book of Revelation was written before 70 A.D. and therefore its prophecies were about the destruction of Jerusalem in that year.

Response: For the Preterist position to maintain any sense of reality, the assertion that the book of Revelation was written before 70 A.D. is a necessary one. Being as the preterist position teaches that the events predicted in the book of Revelation were all fulfilled in 70 A.D., (in the preterist view, up through chapter 19 was fulfilled by 70 A.D., and chapter 20 is the church age) the book of Revelation, from their view, could not have been written after that time. Otherwise the prophecies would have been fulfilled before they were even written!

There are very serious difficulties with attempts to prove such an early writing of Revelation. Overwhelmingly, scholars date the writing of the book near the end of the century, 80-90 A.D. One reason for this is that a number of the first century church fathers attest that this was true, with Irenaeus specifically declaring such to be the case and going so far as to identify its writing with the latter part of Domitian's reign. This places its writing in the last years of the century.

A close reading of the admonitions of chapters 2-3 given to the seven churches of Asia Minor reveals that these churches were already old enough to be taken to task for negative developments within them. These conditions, which would have taken time to develop, reveal that theses local churches had drifted from their beginning commitment to Christ. First love is gone and false doctrines have insinuated themselves. Were the Revelation written before 70 A.D., they would have still been in their infancy, making it difficult to imagine them having time to develop the negative conditions for which they are chastised.

Finally, the book is written, as attested by John himself, while in exile on the isle of Patmos. History records that such persecution of Christians by exile took place under Domitian, which, as noted above, was very late in the first century.

Preterism Claim #5: The book of Revelation, that is, chapters 1-19, have already been fulfilled. (Various events in history are cited as being these fulfillments.) Thus, there is no rapture of the church, no coming Tribulation period, no restoration of national Israel, and no 1000 year Millennium period in which the devil will be bound.

Response: Preterist teaching is that the book of Revelation was fulfilled by 70 A.D. and that Revelation 20:3, which specifies a 1000 year period, should be interpreted allegorically, and, is the church age. The Lord came (in judgment) in 70 A.D. and, thus, is not coming again to catch the church away. There is thus no catching away of the church, no devil unleashed in the world, no Great Tribulation period such as the world has never known, no restoration of Israel and no Millennium.

Attempting to defend such a position demands ignoring literally scores of scriptures, both Old and New Testament, which address these subjects repeatedly, and which simply cannot be explained away. Numerous scriptures have already been cited concerning the devil and his present nefarious work in the earth. Also addressed above is the fact that the 70 A.D. destruction of Jerusalem comes far, far short of qualifying as a great tribulation such as the world has never known. In regards to denying the restoration of Israel, dozens of Old Testament scriptures must be disregarded or allegorized. In addition, New Testament passages must also be disregarded, including such as the following:

> *For I would not have you ignorant brethren, that ye should be ignorant of this mystery, lest ye should be wise in your*

*own conceits; that blindness in part is happened to Israel,
until the fulness of the Gentiles be come in. And so all Israel
shall be saved: as it is written, There shall come out of Sion
the Deliverer, and shall turn away ungodliness from Jacob:
For this is my covenant unto them, when I shall take away
their sins. As concerning the gospel, they are enemies for
your sakes: but as touching the the election, they are beloved
for the fathers' sakes For the gifts and callings of God are
without repentance.*

–Romans 11:25-29

Preterism Claim #6: For some preterists, the idea of rightly dividing the Word of God by identifying the epochal shifts which have been identified as "dispensations" is a lie produced by Christian hating Jews in collaboration and conspiracy with Gentile Masons.

Response: The idea of "dispensations" is totally unacceptable to the preterist position. Few subjects receive more resistance. To accept that these scriptural, progressive, movements exist in scripture is tantamount to complete dismantling of the preterist position. Therefore preterism looks upon the teaching of dispensations as non-scriptural and a product of the late 19th century.

The truth is that, regardless of what term is used to describe these transitional periods, they clearly exist in scripture. To deny that there are major transitions as to the distinctives of how God's grace was dispensed to man, for example, before the Fall in Eden and after, is unrealistic. Or, to deny that there is major transition at the time of the Flood, or at Babel with the confusion of languages and the call of Abraham, or at the giving of the Law at Sinai, or at Calvary and Pentecost--these are clearly and undeniably epochal scriptural transitions which cannot be honestly ignored or categorized as insignificant. They are, in fact, major, unavoidable markers in scripture. What they clearly are *not* is some conspiracy from hell-inspired Jews to confuse the church.

Preterism Claim #7: At least some who hold the preterist position are not sure whether this age will ever end, or simply continue forever. At any rate, according to the preterism, the idea that there is coming a thousand year millennium period when Christ will reign on earth is neither scriptural nor something that was taught throughout church history, but is a creation of 1800's dispensational teaching.

Response: The preterist position is often unclear on what the future holds--sometimes asserting that maybe this age will simply go on forever--even though this is in direct contrast to many scriptures. Indeed, the church has this hope:

> *Behold I shew you a mystery; We shall not all sleep, but we shall all be changed. In a moment, in the twinkling of an eye, at the last trump: for the trumpet shall sound, and the dead shall be raised incorruptible, and we shall be changed*
> –I Cor. 15:51-52

Further, the idea of consecutive time periods, or that the church age will be followed by a millennial period of Christ's return and reign on earth is not the product of 1800's dispensationalism but has been taught, not only throughout church history but is found in the teachings of major religions in general as well as in Christianity throughout the ages. Arnold Ehlert in his book, A Bibliographic History of Dispensationalism, thoroughly documents that the idea of man's earth history ending with a 1000 year period is ingrained deeply in ancient history as well as modern.[48] Below is a sample of some of those who taught a millennial kingdom to come.

- The Jewish tradition of the 6000 years, followed by the Sabbath Millennium, dates at least from the second century B.C., the approximate date of Rabbi Elias from which comes "the tradition of the house of Elias." He taught that the world would be "2000 years void of the law, 2000 years under the law, with a following 2000 years followed by a seventh millennium in which "the earth would be renewed and the righteous dead raised' that these should not again be turned to dust, and that the just then alive should mount up with wings as the eagle…"

- The author of *Cespar Mishna*, in his notes on Maimonides, writes: "At the end of 6000 years will be the day of judgment, and it will also be the Sabbath, the beginning of the world to come. The Sabbath year, and year of Jubilee, intend the same thing."

- RabbI Ketina is quoted from the Gemarah, a comment on the Mishna, to the effect that, "in the last of the thousands of years of the world's continuance, the world shall be destroyed;…even as every seventh year is a year of release, so of the seventh thousand years of the world, it shall be the thousand years of release."

- Among the earliest Christian writings, the Epistle of Barnabas (70-79 A.D.) states: "And even in the beginning of the creation he makes mention of the Sabbath. And God made in six days the works of his hands; and he finished them on the seventh day, and he rested the seventh day, and sanctified it. Consider, my children, what that signifies, he finished them in six days. The meaning of it is this; that in six thousand years the Lord God will bring all things to an end. For with him one day is a thousand years; as himself testifieth, saying, Behold this day shall be as a thousand years. Therefore, children, in six days, that is, in six thousand years, shall all things be accomplished. And what is that he saith, And he rested the seventh day; he meaneth this; that when his Son shall come, and abolish the season of the Wicked One, and judge the ungodly; and shall change the sun, and the moon, and the stars; then he shall gloriously rest in that seventh day."

- Justin Martyr (100-167), Irenaeus (130-?), Hippolytus (200's) Cyprian (200-258), Lactantius (260-340) Hilary, Bishop of

Poitiers (300-367)--these and many more all taught that the days of creation created a scheme of 6 successive periods of human history, followed by a seventh of a thousand years. Jerome, translator of the Latin Vulgate Bible "taught that the world would endure but 6,000 years, and at their termination the consummation would occur, and Christ come." Barnabas, Papias, Tertullian, Commodian, Mathias, and Polycarp were also premillenialists.[49] The list could go on. While this does not mean that we would consider all quoted here as being correct in all of their doctrines, it does mean that the teaching that a thousand year millennium is coming is certainly not a new teaching. Premillennialism can be traced back to the early history of the church and beyond. Historic premillennialism could be defined simply as the belief based on an interpretation of Revelation 20:1-10, that there will be an earthly reign of Christ following his second coming.[50]

Dispensations And British-Israelism

The second error is national or ethnic groups which claim that they are the authentic Jews. Of course, this makes those in the nation of Israel which claim to be Jews as not being true Jews—and, in fact, some preterist as well as British-Israel teaching is that they should be opposed for being deceivers and liars. The scores of Old Testament scriptures which clearly and distinctly outline literally hundreds of promises to Israel are discarded or re-applied to the particular group making such claims. In both preterism and British-Israelism national Israel, to whom scores of unconditional, everlasting promises were made, is replaced. As previously noted, in the event these Old Testament promises don't seem to fit the church (in the first case) or the groups which claim that they, in fact, are the Jews, such scriptures are then interpreted as being "allegorical." More often than not the secret to interpreting these allegories lies with some special person(s) who have supposedly received a "special" revelation.

British-Israelism is actually only one form of a doctrinal error of any group which appropriates for itself the, earthly, natural and political identity and promises given to natural Israel, with all the blessings attached thereto. Numerous other "non-British" groups have also done this. However, British-Israelism is probably the largest form of this teaching. One of the results of such claims is the demonization of natural Jews, which are presented as being impostors. Of course like all doctrines, these beliefs have far-reaching consequences.

The "British-Israelism" form of this doctrine is the teaching that the English people are the actual Jews and that Ephraim and Manasseh is England and the United States. The British Empire is the fulfillment of scriptures which promise Israel dominion over islands of the sea and other nations. This is a national doctrine of the nation of England.

The Church of England is thus a state church, that is, is supported and sponsored by the state. To those believing they are natural Israel as well as spiritual, this nation-as-church idea seems only natural, being as Old Testament Israel obviously had only one government as well as one religious organization.

The main church edifice in England is Westminster Abbey, which sits across the street from Parliament and other government buildings. Each end of the church has large stain glass windows, one containing likenesses of the twelve patriarchs of the Old Testament, the other containing likenesses of the twelve apostles of the New Testament. Buried within the edifice itself are many of England's famous citizens. Of course, to be a hero for the nation was tantamount to being a biblical hero, and thus it seemed obviously appropriate that these should be interred in the church.

In the middle of the edifice is a throne-like seat which sits over a rather large stone. This stone is purported to be a stone which was originally in the land of Israel, and was the actual stone used for the coronation of Israel's ancient kings. The story goes that, when Israel went into exile Jeremiah and/or Baruch brought this very stone to England around the 5th century B.C. (Our research, using English literature, was able to trace an actual history of the stone only back to approximately 1000 A.D. although earliest records of a church where Westminster Abbey now sits goes back to about 785 A.D.)

The idea that a particular earthly, national people is actually the Jewish nation carries with it numerous implications. Historically, those who espoused such have positioned themselves as the chosen elite, the natural outgrowth of which has often been a sense of mission as well as superiority. Adolf Hitler used a variation of this in presenting Germany as a superior chosen people. Through the years numerous militia groups in America—including many Ku Klux Klansmen—also espouse this idea. For many, the existing United States government is actually "anti-christ" and the particular militia group is the "Israel of God" and is thus divinely authorized as a representative of the true believers. Under this arrangement everything from insurrection to refusing to pay taxes to the government is justified. Further, being as the select people is God's people, elitism and a variety of forms of prejudice also emerge.

As is evident from the above, the appropriation of Israel's natural promises to the church has serious and aberrant consequences. Having the necessity of finding a way to apply to their particular group the many Old Testament earthly promises given natural Israel, a wide variety of schemes, some of them verging on the fantastic, have been developed over time.

The fact is that the church is not a political body whose present purpose is political control or power in the world. Nor is it any specific nationality, color, or race. The Spirit works silently in the individual hearts of all men in disregard of all such finite distinctions. The early church, while wrestling with the question of present purpose of the church age, discerned that this purpose is neither to establish natural Israel nor to establish Christ's political control upon earth, but rather is clearly stated in Acts:

> *Simeon hath declared how God at the first did visit the Gentiles, to take out of them a people for his name.*
>
> –Acts 15:14

Thus the church is not a present day political body. It is not a specific nation within the ranks of the nations of the world. It is not a specific race or nationality. Rather the church is the body of Christ. It is God taking out of the Gentiles a people for his name, after which time he shall return to bring to fruition the promises made to earthly Israel.

Dispensational Teaching and Covenant Theology

Covenant Theology and Dispensational Teaching are two dissimilar systems of theology which attempt to explain the plan of God for salvation from sin, the place of Israel and the Church in that plan, and the relationship of Israel to the Church in the present and in the future. The principles used to interpret the biblical text are the difference between Covenant Theology and Dispensational Teaching.

The Renaissance of the fourteenth through seventeenth centuries saw the revival of classical influences in art and literature, and the beginning of modern science in Medieval Europe.[51] Medieval Theology was demonstrated by "Scholasticism" which viewed theology from a philosophical stance and not from a scriptural viewpoint.[52] The allegorical method assumed that figurative language provided a deeper spiritual meaning but failed to develop sound literally interpreted doctrines. After the Renaissance, the call for a factual, more literal understanding of the sciences brought about a dynamic change for theological development.

In the church world, the prominent system of biblical interpretation is a literal hermeneutic identified as the Grammatical-Historical method. As its name indicates, it is a study of grammar and the examination of the historical context. In this vein, the dispensational hermeneutic employs a literal approach to explain scripture by considering every word in its normal and customary meaning. This literal method of interpretation allows the use of symbolism and figures of speech, because of their normal and customary place in every-day language. However, for dispensational teaching, figurative language is for the intent of communicating literal concepts.[53]

Therefore, dispensational teaching follows a literal interpretation of biblical text, including prophetic utterances. They recognize the distinctions between the overall program God has for Israel and the church. Dispensational Theology concludes that the ultimate goal is to restore to the glory of God a universe that is free from rebellion and sin, *"that God may be all in all,"* I Cor. 15:28.

Covenant Theologians are in agreement with the necessity for a literal method of interpretation. However, they lack consistency when reading symbolic and apocalyptic passages. First, their conviction is that there are deeper meanings to be found by spiritualizing a text. Second, their belief in a "one people of God" prohibits a literal future fulfillment of prophecy for Israel. A core element of Covenant Theology is to interpret the Bible through two governing categories--the covenant of works and the covenant of grace. Another element is the propensity to read the New Testament blessings into the Old Testament promises. Third, salvation is the ultimate purpose and driving principle of Covenant Theology.

These two hermeneutical systems each have a discernable theory for establishing biblical unity and the explanation of its progressive truth. Covenant Theology stresses that the Old Testament promises to Israel are all being fulfilled at this time in the elect people, that is, the church, of the New Testament. In contrast, the stance of Dispensational Theology acknowledges that the Old Testament promises have not all been fulfilled, but will be completed at a future date. The Reformers were the first to represent theology in a sense of two major covenants. The beginning of Covenant Theology is credited to Coccius, a reformed theologian (1603-1669.)[54] "Covenant Theology is the system of theology that centers on God as a covenant-making God and sees in the history of creation two great covenants."[55] These are labeled the Covenant of Works before the fall and the Covenant of Grace after the transgression in the Garden in Eden. The Westminster Confession of A.D. 1647 defined the boundaries and distinguishing features of this proposed unifying and redemptive concept of covenant. "The first covenant made with man was a covenant of works, wherein life was promised to Adam, and, in him, to his posterity, upon condition of perfect and personal obedience. Man by his fall having made himself incapable of life by that covenant, the Lord was pleased to make a second, commonly called the Covenant of Grace: whereby he freely offereth unto sinners life and salvation by Jesus Christ requiring of them faith in him, that they may be saved; and promising to give unto all those that are ordained unto life His Holy Spirit, to make them willing and able to believe.[56] Covenant Theology became the regulating rule for biblical interpretation in the Calvinist's official soteriology.

REFORM THEOLOGY

Reform Theology stresses the doctrine of John Calvin and Ulrich Zwingli, which is the Calvinistic approach and distinct from Lutheranism. The reform tradition emphasizes God's sovereignty and has more to do with individual salvation (Calvinism-Tulip) than with the church or the doctrines of the last days. As already noted, reformed theology is represented by two covenant categories, identified as the Covenant of Works, and the Covenant of Grace.

COVENANT THEOLOGY

The theological covenants are conjectures that were instituted during the reformation. The Covenants of Works (Genesis 2:16-17; Hosea 6:7; Romans 5:12-17) and Grace (Genesis 3:15; 17:7; Jeremiah 31:33; II Cor. 6:16-18; Rev. 21:3), established by the Reformers, are not biblical covenants. They are based on theological assumptions assembled from theological concepts taken from many remote and isolated text citations.

The first covenant of Covenant Theology is the Covenant of Works that can, at best, only be implied from Genesis 2:15-17. This covenant is assumed and is derived from the Edenic responsibility "thou shalt not," along with the specific "thou shalt surely die" condition. The assumption is that, had Adam, as representative of the human race, obeyed the "shalt not" injunction, he would have continued in eternal life. However, "no explicit promise of eternal life was ever given to Adam before the fall."[57]

The second covenant of Covenant Theology is defined as the Covenant of Grace. Reformed theologians described this as the plan of God for fulfilling His promises. This supposed Covenant of Grace began at the fall and is concluded at the second advent of Christ. This declaration allows Covenant Theology to offer the same salvation foundation throughout human history, that is, salvation by faith in Christ. The important feature of this idea is the continuation of the elect as the one people of God throughout history. The elect people of God (Isa. 45:4; Romans 22:5; I Peter1:2), in the Old Testament begins with Adam after the Fall and continues to Israel, the church in the wilderness, (Acts 7:38.) The New Testament church and the Old Testament elect constitute the one people of God, (Exodus 6:7; Psalms 28:9; Gal. 6:16.) The result is that the distinction between Israel and the church is obscured.

Usually, Covenant and Reform Theology are interchangeable, but the particular architecture of Covenant Theology is sometimes expressed by an additional theological covenant. This additional third covenant, linked to the works-grace covenants, is termed the Covenant of Redemption. The Covenant of Redemption states that at some time the Trinity of God entered into a mutual agreement that the Father would give His "only begotten Son" (John 3:16) as a sacrifice for sin. The Son, in "the fullness of time" (Gal. 4:4) would willingly take on the form of a human to die on the Cross as man's substitute (I Peter 2:24.) The Holy Ghost vowed to the Father and the Son that he would "reprove the world of sin" (John 16:8) and provide eternal life to reconciled man. The Father pledged a reward to His "anointed servant" for enduring the travail of reconciliation, (Isa. 53:ll; Heb. 12:2.) This covenant is, of necessity, based on theological constructs which were created long after New Testament writings, and cannot be identified in scripture.

Covenant Theology emphasizes the unity and uniformity of scripture and of God's people whether Old or New Testament. It claims one salvation, one general resurrection, and one general final judgment. It should be remembered, in conclusion, that the hermeneutic method of determining the purpose and meaning of God's plan is allegorical and depends on figurative and symbolic interpretations.

This method of spiritualizing literal statements emerges from a pattern of two or three theological covenants that have no scriptural basis as a covenant. Their merit is solely on the conceived idea that these covenants are the proper instruments to guide men into salvation from sin and to identify the place of Israel and the Church in God's plan as understood from His promises, especially noting the relation of national Israel with today's church.

Dispensational Theology

A dispensation is a period of time that emphasizes God's governing and superintending of the human family. It is a special segment of time based on a continuing and progressively unfolding revelation of God that is the basis for the administration of life and stewardship. Each dispensation is tested and human failure is judged accordingly.

Dispensational teaching relates to biblical covenants as they pertain to the promise of Genesis 3:15. These covenants are:

1. Abrahamic
2. Davidic
3. Palestinian
4. New Covenant

Distinctions between Israel and the church are maintained. The promises made to the House of Israel will be completely fulfilled in the regathered national Israel. The century long resurgence of national Israel, consummated with the birth of Israel as a nation in 1948 is not important to a covenant theologian, but it is significant for dispensational interpretation. Dispensationalists teach that today is the day of the Church and that day will close with the secret rapture of the believing righteous.

Dispensational teaching places much more emphasis on a literal interpretation of the Old Testament than do Covenant Theologians. Dispensational theology concludes that discrediting the literalness of the Old Testament creates chaos and distorts the soundness of the Old Testament. For one to interpret the Old Testament's literal promises in another manner would not be agreeable or compatible with the divine witness. The biblically-based Old Testament covenants of promise (Eph. 2:12) from Abraham onward are addressed to Israel. The Abrahamic, Davidic, Palestinian, and New Covenant have not been completed. While the Church is presently the recipient of these spiritual promises, they will, at some future date, be literally and spiritually fulfilled in national Israel. The time of their literal fulfillment will follow the Tribulation period and begins with the Second Coming of Christ.

COMPARISONS OF COVENANT THEOLOGY AND DISPENSATIONAL TEACHING

	COVENANT THEOLOGY	DISPENSATIONAL TEACHING
STRUCTURE	Based on contrived theological covenants: • "Works" with Adam • "Grace" with Christ • "Redemption" with the Trinity of God • God's program is allegedly revealed through these assumed theological covenants	Scripture identifies seven periods of time, revealing salvation and stewardship, based on the progressive revelation of God and his purpose. • Innocence: Pre-fall • Conscience: Post-fall • Human Government: Noah • Promise: Abraham (Patriarchs) • Law: Moses • Grace: Church (First Advent) • Kingdom: Millennium (Second Advent) God's program is determined through separate, progressive, dispensations.
SOTERIOLOGIC PLATFORM	Ultra-Calvinism, normally five-point: • Total depravity • Unconditional election • Limited atonement • Irresistible grace • Perseverance of the saints	Armenian or Calvinist, rarely an Ultra-Calvinist. (See author's book, "Grace" is a Pentecostal word)
VIEW OF BIBLICAL COVENANTS	Biblical covenants are in conjunction with the assumed covenants of works and grace, (and sometimes the added covenant of redemption.)	Biblical covenants highlight and basically parallel dispensations in which God's specific requirements progress toward the ultimate fulfillment.
PROGRESSIVE REVELATION	Presupposes that the governing principle of God's plan is the Covenant of Grace. Begins with Adam and continues until the White Throne Judgment.	God's design for the human race was gradually unfolded as history progressed. The new dispensation does not contradict earlier ones. Each new dispensational revelation is sequential and amplifies God's purpose until "its completion."

	COVENANT THEOLOGY	DISPENSATIONAL TEACHING
UNIFYING FACTOR	The single purpose of God is to save God's predetermined elect. One people of God, the Gentile Church, is the "new" elect Israel of God. Natural Israel has been permanently set aside because of unbelief, and replaced forever by the New Testament elect and the Jewish remnant that expresses faith in Christ.	The single purpose of God is to save "whosoever will." Israel is a chosen, earthly nation and the Church is a chosen "heavenly" people (Heb. 12:18-23, 28), two distinct groups of the people of God, having different destinies but ultimately defined as "one new man" (Eph. 2:15) Israel has a special future with God in a restored environment during the literal one-thousand year period.
USE OF SCRIPTURE (Hermeneutic)	(Allegorical) The New Testament is used to interpret the Old Testament. All Old Testament prophesies of a restored Israel are to be applied allegorically to the Church.	(Literal) The Old Testament provides insight into New Testament interpretation. The Old Testament promises made to Israel are to be taken literally.
THEOLOGICAL DISSIMILARITIES CONCERNING THE PROMISE	The primary recipient of the benefit of Abraham's covenant was Christ and "spiritual Israel." Maintains the understanding that there is a theological Covenant of Redemption made by the trinity of God to effect the elect is essential to reveal the redemptive purpose. Expresses a supposed theological covenant of works, with Adam as an unmovable precursor to the covenant of Grace. God made a specific Covenant of Grace with Christ that includes the elect--even Adam.	The primary recipients of Abraham's covenant are both natural Israel and the Church. Contests the reliability of the Theological Covenant of Redemption that was supposedly entered into by the persons of the trinity to restore fallen mankind. Reject the theological assumption that Adam in the garden of Eden entered into a covenant of works with God. The supposed theological Covenant of Grace lacks scriptural authentication and is, therefore, unsatisfactory and misleading.

	COVENANT THEOLOGY	DISPENSATIONAL TEACHING
THE CHURCH	Israel was, and is, the church (elect) in the wilderness (Acts 7:38) and it was good. However, the church was improved in the New Testament with an elect remnant of Israel and Gentiles that had faith in Christ. The church will reach its best in the Utopia of the New Heavens and New Earth. Because Israel is the Church, Old Testament prophecies concerning the church are assumed to be many. Covenant ministries allegorically apply Old Testament standards to the New Testament Church. The Church, from it's beginning in the Old Testament, is the product and conclusion of God's saving purpose for the elect. All believers in every age are "in Christ" and are members of the "body of Christ" -- the one church. The foundation for the Church finds its structure in the Old Testament scriptures.	The Church, as a distinct entity, was birthed on the Day of Pentecost, and will be completed at the Rapture. Prophecies by Old Testament prophets to Israel were not primarily and specifically to the Church. The Church is a period of time in history in which God's dealing with the Gentile nations while Israel, as God's chosen, remains in unbelief (Rom. 11:25.) Believers of the Old Testament are not in the church, the body of Christ, as that is reserved for those participating in the Mystery Kingdom of God, John 3:2-7; Matt. 13.
ISRAEL AND THE CHURCH	The Israel of God, found in Gal. 6:16, means the Church is spiritual Israel.	Spiritual Israel is physical Jews that are in the Church that have been spiritually blessed with the New Testament baptism of the Holy Ghost, which is the fulfillment of the New Covenant. (Jer. 31:31-34)
OLD TESTAMENT PROPHECY	Applied only to the Church (God's people)	Even though the Church has received spiritual promises first given to Israel, this does not negate their future fulfillment to the nation of Israel.
CHURCH AGE	Simply a continuation of reconciliation, which unfolds for the elect throughout history from the Old Testament into The New.	There is a "time gap" wherein National Israel is set aside while God is calling out a people for His Name (Church.) (Acts 15:14-17)

	COVENANT THEOLOGY	DISPENSATIONAL TEACHING
THE MILLENNIUM	***"Amillennialism"** (William E Cox)[58]* Usually amillennial with some post-millennial. (Millennium is spiritual, not literal.) The Millennium is a spiritual Kingdom that began at the Christ's birth and ends at the Second Coming. Christ sits on throne as Saints rule with Him (this is spiritual during this present age.) The throne is not literal. It is symbolic of power and authority. Israel entered the promised land under Joshua and lost it to the nations because of persistent unbelief and disobedience. The Land will not be restored to Israel. God has no future dealings with Israel. Satan was bound by Christ at the First Advent. Being "bound" here means "spiritually limited." Christ abolished Old Testament sacrifices	***Literal Millennium*** Are pre-Millennial, usually with pre-Tribulation rapture. The Millennium is a literal, earthly reign of Christ of one-thousand years duration. It is the time when Israel shall experience the New Covenant. (Jer. 31:31-34.) Messiah, the "Son of David," will literally sit on the throne in Jerusalem and rule ethnic Israel and the world with Israel as the head of the nations. The land deeded to Abraham and his descendents by God will become their possession again as God gathers Israel from the nations at the end of the age just as he repeatedly promised. Satan will be literally bound in the Bottomless Pit during the one-thousand year period (removed; no activity.) Old Testament sacrifices may be restored to a "memorial" to Christ's finished work.
THE SECOND ADVENT	Literal return at the end of the spiritual millennium; all eyes shall see Him. There is no way to determine when.	Literal return immediately before the millennium; all eyes shall see Him. Signs point the way to the nearness of His coming.
THE RESURRECTION	There is one literal "general resurrection." The "first resurrection" is spiritual; from dead in sin to walk in newness of life. The Second Coming marks the General Resurrection of all people in every generation, both the elect and the lost.	The First Resurrection is literal and takes place in phases: "For each man shall stand in his lot at the end of the days," Daniel 12:12. Christ calls out *the Church* at the Rapture. The *Old Testament* saints are resurrected at the second literal return of Christ. *The lost await* the Second Resurrection after Satan is loosed for a short season following the Millennium. This is The "White Throne" judgment "Every man in his own order," I Cor. 15:22-23

	COVENANT THEOLOGY	DISPENSATIONAL TEACHING
THE JUDGMENT	The Lord's return with His saints will immediately begin the General (Final) Judgment. At this time the elect and the lost will face their different judgments: The elect for eternal rewards The lost for determining one's degree of eternal punishment This event closes the present age.	Immediately after the Rapture, the Church in Heaven will be judged for their individual rewards (Bema), Also, at the Marriage Supper of the Lamb, the bride will be united with the Bridegroom in eternal perfection and glory. Following this is the Second Coming to judge the nations and establish Israel in a literal Millennium. All the wicked will be resurrected to the Second Death judgment just prior to the renovation of the earth by fire. This occurs at the end of the millennium.
THE FINAL STATE –IMMORTALITY	Is an endless duration of life with God-no physical death. It will be consummated at the Second Advent.	Begins an endless life with God for: The Church at the rapture. The Old Testament saints at the second coming. Others in their own time and order.
THE NEW HEAVENS AND THE NEW EARTH	The earth will not be annihilated but renovated. This takes place immediately following the events that accompany and follow the Second Advent. The new earth is cleansed and made ready for the Elect, the one people of God of all time.	The earth is renovated by fire; following the Millennium. The descent of the new Jerusalem; The pure river of life; The throne of God and the Lamb shall be here. There is no night there.

Endnotes

1 Lint, G. (Ed.) (1990). *The Complete Biblical Library* (Vol. 14, (p. 382). Springfield, MO: World Library Press.

2 Christensen, D. (1996). *Bible 101* (p. xiv). N. Richland Hills, TX: Bible Press.

3 Wellard, J. (1972). *Babylon* (p. 91). New York, NY: Saturday Review Press.

4 Nelson, R.D. (2006). *From Eden to Babel* (pp. 131, 132). St. Louis MO: Chalice Press.

5 ibid. 308.

6 Tablet VII Column IV, from the ancient Royal Assyrian Library, about 2200 B.C.: Smith, G. (1876). *Dept. of Oriental Antiquities, British Museum, The Chaldean Account of Genesis* (p. 227). New York, NY: Scribner, Armstrong & Co.

7 Budge, E.A.W (1925). *Babylonian Life and History* (p. 64). London, England: The Religious Tract Society.

8 ibid. 181.

9 *Athenaeum*, Feb. 12, 1876.

10 *Memoires de l'Institut*, (Vol. xxxix). (pp. 293ff).

11 ibid.

12 ibid. 311.

13 ibid. 110.

14 ibid. 145.

15 ibid. 149.

16 ibid. 150.

17 ibid. 212, 151.

18 Larue, G.A. (1969). *Babylon and the Bible* (pp. 14-17). Grand Rapids, MI: Baker Book House.

19 ibid. 311.

20 Dumbrell, W.J. (1984). *Covenant and Creation, A Theology of Old Testament Covenants,* (p. 15). Nashville, TN: Thomas Nelson Publishers.

21 Schmertz, C.M. (1995). *The Covenant Symbol, a thesis* (p. 1). Berkeley, CA: Graduate Theological Union.

22 Ricoeur, P. (1976) *Interpretation Theory: Discourse and the Surplus of Meaning* (p. 178). Fort Worth, TX: Texas Christian University Press.

23 Reiner, E.W. (1967) *The Covenants* (pp. 21, 22). Nashville, TN: Southern Publishing Association.

24 McComiskey, T.E. (1985). *The Covenants of Promise* (p. 62). Grand Rapids, MI: Baker Book House.

25 Eichrodt, W. (1961). Theology of the Old Testament, (vol. 1, p. 37). Philadelphia, Westminster: J.A. Baker.

26 Matthews, V.H. (2000). *Old Testament Themes* (pp. 17, 18). St. Louis, MO: Chalice Press

27 Ratzliff, J. (1999). *Many Religions, One Covenant* (p. 59). San Francisco, CA: Ignatius Press.

28 Lewis Sperry Chafer, quoted in:
Cox, W.E. (1963). *An examination of dispensationalism,* Philadelphia, PA: Presbyterian and Reformed Publishing Co.

29 ibid. 49-50.

30 Mauro, P. (1928). *The Gospel of the Kingdom* London, England: Hamilton Brothers.

31   Saucy, R.L. (1993). *The Case for Progressive Dispensationalism*, Grand Rapids, MI: Zondervan Publishing House.

32   Pettingill, W.L. *Bible Questions Answered* (p. 112). Grand Rapids, MI: Zondervan Publishing.

33   Berkhof, L. (1941). *Systematic Theology* (pp. 293, 301). Grand Rapids, MI: Wm. B. Eerdmans Publishing Co.

34   Ryrie, C.C. (1965). *Dispensationalism Today* (p. 15). Chicago IL: Moody Press.

35   Ramm, Bernard L. (1956). *Protestant Biblical Interpretation*, (rev. ed., p. 158). Boston, MA: W.A. Wilde.

36   Ladd, G.E. (1952). *Crucial Questions About the Kingdom of God*. Grand Rapids, MI: Wm. B. Eerdmans Publishing Co.

37   Mauro 8-9.

38   Ladd

39   Ehlert, A.D. (1965). *A Bibliographic History of Dispensationalism*. Grand Rapids, MI: Baker Book House.

40   Cave, W. (1675) *The Lives of the Apostles* (3rd ed., Revised, pp. 1-106). Oxford, 1840.

41   Poiret, P., *The Divine Economy, An Universal System of the Works and Purpose of God Towards Men Demonstrated* (7 volumes in 4). (as bound in the edition in the Rufus M. Jones Collection on Mysticism at Haverford College, the last volume having been labeled Volume VII. London, 1713. See especially Vol. III, pp. 150).

42   Edwards, J. (1699). *A Compleat History or Survey of all the Dispensations and Methods of Religion* (2 Volumes) London, England.

43   Barrington, J.S. (1826). *Theological Works* (Vol. II, pp. 379, 380, 387). London, England.

44   Leeds, (1753). *7-volume edition of Watts' Works* (Vol. II, pp. 625-660, 537-553). London, England. –as quoted by Ehlert.

45   Edwards, J. A, *History of the work of Redemption, Evangelical Family Library* (Vol. IX, p. 16). New York, N.Y. –as quoted by Ehlert.

46   Fletcher, J. (1836). *John Fletcher's Works* (Vol. II, p. 261). –as quoted by Ehlert.

47   Darby, J.N., *The Collected Writings of J.N. Darby, (1857-1867)* (Second Edition, Vol. I, pp. 192, 193). London, England.

48   Ehlert

49   Jackson, S.C. (1918). *The Millennial Hope* (pp. 171-174). Chicago, IL: University of Chicago Press.

50   Cox 3.

51   *Webster's Encyclopedic Unabridged Dictionary of the English Language.* (1989). New York, NY: Gramercy Books.

52   Ennis P. (1989). *The Moody Handbook of Theology* (p. 404). Chicago, IL: Moody Press.

53   ibid. 520-21.

54   Erickson, J. (2001). *The Concise Dictionary of Christian Theology* (p. 37). Wheaton, IL: Crossway Books.

55   Grentz, J., GuretzkI D., & Nordling, C.F. (1999). *Pocket Dictionary of Theological Terms* (p. 32). Downers Grove, IL: InterVarsity Press.

56   Williamson, G. I. (1964). *The Westminster Confession of Faith for Study Classes* (p. 216). Philadelphia, PA: Presbyterian and Reformed Publishing Company.

57   Berkhof, L. (1998). *Systematic Theology Bath* (p. 216). Great Britain: The Bath Press.

58   Cox

Bibliography

Barrington, J.S. (1826). *Theological Works* (Vol. II). London, England.

Berkhof, L. (1941). *Systematic Theology*. Grand Rapids, MI: Wm. B. Eerdmans Publishing Co.

Berkhof, L. (1998). *Systematic Theology Bath*. Great Britain: The Bath Press.

Budge, E.A.W (1925). *Babylonian Life and History*. London, England: The Religious Tract Society.

Cave, W. (1675) *The Lives of the Apostles* (3rd ed., Revised). Oxford, 1840.

Christensen, D. (1996). *Bible 101*. N. Richland Hills, TX: Bible Press.

Cox, W.E. (1963). *An examination of dispensationalism*. Philadelphia, PA: Presbyterian and Reformed Publishing Co.

Darby, J.N., *The Collected Writings of J.N. Darby, (1857-1867)* (Second Edition, Vol. I). London, England.

Dumbrell, W.J. (1984). *Covenant and Creation, A Theology of Old Testament Covenants*. Nashville, TN: Thomas Nelson Publishers.

Edwards, J. (1699). *A Compleat History or Survey of all the Dispensations and Methods of Religion* (2 Volumes). London, England.

Edwards, J. A, *History of the work of Redemption, Evangelical Family Library* (Vol. IX). New York, N.Y.

Eichrodt, W. (1961). Theology of the Old Testament (vol. 1). Philadelphia, Westminster: J.A. Baker.

Ehlert, A.D. (1965). *A Bibliographic History of Dispensationalism*. Grand Rapids, MI: Baker Book House.

Ennis P. (1989). *The Moody Handbook of Theology*. Chicago, IL: Moody Press.

Erickson, J. (2001). *The Concise Dictionary of Christian Theology*. Wheaton, IL: Crossway Books.

Fletcher, J. (1836). *John Fletcher's Works* (Vol. II).

Grentz, J., GuretzkI D., & Nordling, C.F. (1999). *Pocket Dictionary of Theological Terms*. Downers Grove, IL: InterVarsity Press.

Jackson, S.C. (1918). *The Millennial Hope*. Chicago, IL: University of Chicago Press.

Ladd, G.E. (1952). *Crucial Questions About the Kingdom of God*. Grand Rapids, MI: Wm. B. Eerdmans Publishing Co.

Larue, G.A. (1969). *Babylon and the Bible*. Grand Rapids, MI: Baker Book House.

Leeds, (1753). *7-volume edition of Watts' Works* (Vol. II). London, England.

Lint, G. (Ed.) (1990). *The Complete Biblical Library* (Vol. 14). Springfield, MO: World Library Press.

Matthews, V.H. (2000). *Old Testament Themes*. St. Louis, MO: Chalice Press

Mauro, P. (1928). *The Gospel of the Kingdom* London, England: Hamilton Brothers.

McComiskey, T.E. (1985). *The Covenants of Promise*. Grand Rapids, MI: Baker Book House.

Nelson, R.D. (2006). *From Eden to Babel*. St. Louis MO: Chalice Press.

Pettingill, W.L. *Bible Questions Answered*. Grand Rapids, MI: Zondervan Publishing.

Poiret, P., *The Divine Economy, An Universal System of the Works and Purpose of God Towards Men Demonstrated* (7 volumes in 4)

Ramm, Bernard L. (1956). *Protestant Biblical Interpretation*, (rev. ed.). Boston, MA: W.A. Wilde.

Ratzliff, J. (1999). *Many Religions, One Covenant*. San Francisco, CA: Ignatius Press.

Reiner, E.W. (1967) *The Covenants*. Nashville, TN: Southern Publishing Association.

Ricoeur, P. (1976) *Interpretation Theory: Discourse and the Surplus of Meaning*. Fort Worth, TX: Texas Christian University Press.

Ryrie, C.C. (1965). *Dispensationalism Today*. Chicago IL: Moody Press.

Saucy, R.L. (1993). *The Case for Progressive Dispensationalism*, Grand Rapids, MI: Zondervan Publishing House.

Schmertz, C.M. (1995). *The Covenant Symbol, a thesis*. Berkeley, CA: Graduate Theological Union.

Smith, G. (1876). *Dept. of Oriental Antiquities, British Museum, The Chaldean Account of Genesis*. New York, NY: Scribner, Armstrong & Co.

Webster's Encyclopedic Unabridged Dictionary of the English Language. (1989) New York, NY: Gramercy Books.

Wellard, J. (1972). *Babylon*. New York, NY: Saturday Review Press.

Williamson, G. I. (1964). *The Westminster Confession of Faith for Study Classes*. Philadelphia, PA: Presbyterian and Reformed Publishing Company.